ENGLISH MADE FOR YOU

an EFL TEXTBOOK

by Rebecca Starr, Ph D

with Illustrations by Leana Wagner

Shinasa

English Made for You

an EFL Textbook

by Rebecca Starr, Ph. D

First Published August 2010
SHINASA Publishing Co.
28-36 NokBeon-Dong, EunPyung-Gu, Seoul, Korea
Registered : 9-52 (Jan. 5 1956)
Tel : 02-382-6411
Fax : 02-382-6401
E-mail : shinasa@chol.com / Homepage : www.shinasa.co.kr

ISBN : 978-89-8396-716-9

Printed in Korea

₩ 13,000

English Made for You

by Rebecca Starr, PhD

Table of Contents

Download mp3 files at publisher's homepage :
www.shinasa.co.kr

Also materials for teachers available.
For more information, please contact.
02-382-6411 / shinasa@chol.com

Acknowledgements

This book is dedicated to Mr. Donald Ferrer, my high school French teacher, and to my students at Won Kwang University. Mr Ferrer set high expectations and made learning a foreign language fun, and I will always be grateful for his structured and dynamic teaching. I want my students to experience the joy of learning a foreign language for its own sake, and to develop confidence in their growing abilities to understand and use English in their daily lives.

For the opportunity to teach in Korea, and for support as I put this book together, I thank Drs. Youngmi Sohn and Yoon-Kyung Yim, Won Kwang University, and my hardworking students. For reading and commenting on the book as a whole, I thank Ana Garza. For additional collegial support, I thank Toni Rudd and Gregory Timlin. I also extend my personal thanks to Paul MacDonald, Ilse Craft, Kate Rycroft, Jane Reid, Glenn Reid, Frank Lopez, Wendy Nomura, Jonathan Utheim, and Andrew Blight, for assistance in preparing the audio files included in the teacher's edition of this book.

INTRODUCTION: About Making the Book

This book is designed for English learners in non-English speaking countries, and in accordance with three fundamental assumptions about how people learn foreign languages. First, people learn more quickly and with greater understanding if the instruction includes the four modes of listening, reading, speaking, and writing together. Second, the vocabulary and forms of the target language are best acquired when the language is taught within particular discourses. Third, student achievement and confidence will best be gained through cumulative learning experiences. Consequently, chapters are arranged so that learning, exercises, and activities are done in tandem, which reinforces the students' understanding of the lesson and their developing fluency. Each successive chapter anticipates mastery of the lesson and vocabulary in the previous chapter. Teaching the chapters as separable modules is likely to impede student success. Student success is measured by the students' abilities to use their knowledge of the forms to anticipate the meaning of forms they've never seen before and to communicate their own thoughts in clear, intelligible English. Although a certain amount of memorization is always helpful when it comes to learning a new language, memorization alone cannot aid students in communicating thought. Indeed, memorization may even dissuade students from learning the meaning of what they are saying.

This book contains twelve chapters and the Teacher's Edition includes four review sections, one to follow after every three chapters. The lessons were selected and arranged to maximize rapid improvement in all four skills. Ideally, this whole book will be used in a sixteen-week, four-unit English course, doing a chapter a week, and spending one week on each review section. The first unit, chapters 1-3, covers word order in simple sentences and commonly used regular and irregular present and past tense verbs. The second unit, chapters 4-6, gives instruction in nouns, pronouns, adjectives and articles, and word order for noun phrases. The third unit, chapters 7-9, discusses questions and polite requests, prepositions and word order for prepositional phrases, and noncountable and collective nouns and nouns that are always plural. The fourth unit, chapter 10-12, includes phrasal verbs, adverbs and transition words, and participles, gerunds, and infinitives.

As I planned this book, I reflected upon the most prevalent types of mistakes I had seen done by second-language learners in my fifteen years of tutoring and teaching college English in America and Korea. I considered, among these error types, which ones were the most unforgivable for a native speaker of English—that is, which ones prevent communication with English speakers and readers. My years of experience told me that meaning in English is produced primarily through word order. Thus, word order had to be the first lesson, and it had to be reinforced throughout the book.

Chapters 3 through 12 are arranged in the following sequence: a dialogue, a vocabulary list divided by parts of speech, a descriptive grammar lesson, a multiple choice exercise, fill-in the blank and / or sentence building exercises, a partner speaking activity, a short reading, reading comprehension questions, and a short writing assignment within the same discourse as the reading. The first two chapters have extended say-back sections and no reading passages, but they do ask students to write sentences. They are structured this way to increase the energy in the classroom and student confidence at the beginning of the semester. The section reviews are designed to test fluency and are therefore timed. Each section review in the Teacher's Edition includes extended multiple choice and sentence-building exercises, reading comprehension questions for the chapter dialogues, dictation exercises which come from the reading passages, and one-on-one speaking tests.

This selection and arrangement of materials is meant to focus students' attention on the forms of English first, to help students get the form in their heads, in their ears, and in their mouths. For this purpose, audio files of the dialogues are available to students at www.shinasa.co.kr. Listen and repeat activities naturalize the sounds for the students so that they can begin to distinguish correct sound from incorrect sound and to detect emotion from tone. Once the grammatical form begins to be imbedded, then the form is explained in a short, simple way and with tables and examples. Several multiple choice exercises give students ample opportunity to begin to distinguish correct form in print and to become confident that they understand the lesson. Multiple choice exercises can be given all at once in class, as homework, or divided between the two. Fill-in and sentence-building exercises ask students to produce the form themselves so that their knowledge becomes active and, as a result, easier for them to remember, produce at a later time, and build on. Partner speaking activities require students to recall the lesson and the vocabulary fairly spontaneously, and master the lesson and the usage for the vocabulary learned. In addition, it is a nice way to break up in-class tasks and offer students opportunities to cooperate with and compete with peers, and to check their progress. The final two parts of chapters 3 through 12, reading comprehension and writing assignments, engage students' abilities in cognitive reflection, which will embed the lesson much deeper. Students need to pay close attention to content and organization, which is a necessary step in the development of fluency.

The review sections are largely designed to hone fluency and are meant to be done in the classroom. Each review begins with a short recap of the lessons in the previous three chapters and then opens to extended exercises covering material with which they are familiar. Mastery of the preceding lessons is indicated when they are challenged to do the work much faster than they did the exercises in the chapters. It is therefore recommended that students be given the same or less time as before to do double the exercises, and timed at the teacher's discretion for the sentence building. These sections include the new task of dictation because dictation is an activity reserved for building fluency, and it is an opportunity to develop higher skills in two modes together, listening and writing. The dictation passages are excerpted from the reading passages at the chapter ends, so students should recognize the vocabulary and grammar, if not some identical sentences.

The lessons in this book make for a very active language-learning classroom and rapid growth toward student fluency in English. They invigorate students and keep their attention on specific vocabulary and functional grammar at the same time. The students quickly develop confidence as they recognize how much English they already know and how fast they can learn and perfect their English abilities. Students appreciate learning lessons about the American lifestyle of the characters in the book, and they learn to enjoy humor in English as they interpret dramatic situations and character motivations in the dialogues. Students also enjoy developing their expressive abilities in writing as they compose e-mails to pen pals, professors, and friends in English. This is of particular importance for students whose native curriculum offers few opportunities to develop verbal skills and critical reasoning in their native language.

I had to write this textbook because I have seen nothing on the market for EFL learners that is based upon the idea that English fluency is acquired through accumulation; nothing that addresses the need to develop listening, speaking, reading, and writing together using the same material and in a balanced way; and nothing that respects and requires student thought and communication in the making and valuing of meaning in the readings and in their lives. As human beings, students enjoy using language to impose their own meanings and values upon the situations, events, and objects in their world. This book gives them the tools and the confidence to do so without limiting their possibilities. It has served my students well beyond my expectations.

CHAPTER 1: In the Kitchen

Grammar

English is a "subject-verb-object" language. This means that most sentences begin with a subject, someone or something that is doing the action. The subject is followed by the verb, or action word. Finally, the verb is followed by the object, or receiver of the action. For example: "The man throws the ball." The subject of this sentence is "the man" because the man is doing the throwing. "Throw" is the verb because it describes the action. The object is "the ball" because the ball receives the action, being thrown.

Dialogue

Dialogue for pronunciation and intonation. The teacher reads to the class, emphasizing pronunciation and intonation. Then the teacher reads Andrea's part while the students read Jill's part. Students pair up and practice the dialogue, and then switch parts and practice again. The teacher corrects pronunciation and intonation.

Andrea	Where is the house?
Jill	The house is on the corner.
Andrea	Who lives there?
Jill	Emma and her family live there.
Andrea	Does Emma have a brother?
Jill	Yes, her brother's name is Henry.
Andrea	Does Emma have a sister?
Jill	Yes, her sister's name is Susan.
Andrea	What are they doing tonight?
Jill	They are making dinner.
Andrea	Who lives next door?
Jill	Mike lives next door.
Andrea	What does Mike make for dinner?
Jill	Mike barbecues a steak for dinner.
Andrea	What does Mike do after dinner?
Jill	He washes the dishes and watches TV.
Andrea	Is Sang-hee going to come over and visit?
Jill	No, Sang-hee is vacuuming the floor tonight.

Names are always capitalized in English.

Vocabulary

✓ Nouns

brother
corner
dinner
dishes
family
floor
house
sister
steak
tonight
TV

✓ Verbs

are
barbecue
come
do
have
is
live
lives
make
vacuum
washes
watches

Spelling Rule. Silent "e." The letter "e" at the end of English words is not pronounced. The silent "e" signals that the vowel that comes before the preceding consonant is long.

Vowel	Words with the long vowel sound:			
Ā	bake	name	pale	state
Ē	delete	obscene	precede	pristine (prĭ – stēn)
Ī	drive	hide	nine	write
Ō	devote	home	robe	smoke
Ū	attitude	consume	cute	tune

Reading. The House. In the sentences below, the subject is italicized, and the verb is underlined.

1. The *woman* bakes a cake.
2. The *man* boils eggs.
3. *Mike* barbecues a steak.
4. *Susan* steams some broccoli.
5. *Mother* answers the phone.
6. *Father* writes an e-mail.
7. *Kim* does her homework.

8. *Darryl* watches TV.
9. *Mother* reads the newspaper.
10. *Todd* washes the dishes.
11. *Sang-hee* vacuums the floor.
12. *Sally* scrubs the bathtub.
13. *Tim* dusts the bookshelf.

➾ Practice saying the sentences.

Sentence Format. All English sentences begin with a capital letter. In addition, all English sentences end with a final punctuation mark, which is usually a period.

Exercise 1.1

Circle the letter in front of the sentence with the correct word order: subject-verb-object.

1. A. Boils the man eggs.
   B. The man boils eggs.
   C. The man eggs boils.
   D. Eggs boils the man.

2. A. The woman the phone answers.
   B. The phone the woman answers.
   C. The woman answers the phone.
   D. The phone answers the woman.

3. A. His homework Tim does.
   B. Tim his homework does.
   C. Does Tim his homework.
   D. Tim does his homework.

4. A. Father washes the dishes.
   B. The dishes wash father.
   C. Wash the dishes father.
   D. Father the dishes washes.

5. A. John a cake bakes.
   B. A cake John bakes.
   C. John bakes a cake.
   D. Bakes John a cake.

6. A. Writes an e-mail Emma.
   B. Emma writes an e-mail.
   C. Emma an e-mail writes.
   D. An e-mail Emma writes.

7. A. TV Carrie watches.
   B. Carrie TV watches.
   C. Carrie watches TV.
   D. Watches Carrie TV.

8. A. Phillip reads the newspaper.
   B. Phillip the newspaper reads.
   C. The newspaper Phillip reads.
   D. Reads Phillip the newspaper.

9. A. Scrubs Sally the bathtub.
   B. Sally the bathtub scrubs.
   C. The bathtub scrubs Sally.
   D. Sally scrubs the bathtub.

10. A. Barbecues Mike a steak.
    B. Mike barbecues a steak.
    C. Mike a steak barbecues.
    D. A steak barbecues Mike.

11. A. Vacuums the floor Sang-hee.
    B. The floor vacuums Sang-hee.
    C. Sang-hee the floor vacuums.
    D. Sang-hee vacuums the floor.

12. A. Christina steams some broccoli.
    B. Some broccoli Christina steams.
    C. Christina some broccoli steams.
    D. Some broccoli steams Christina.

13. A. Andrea the bookshelf dusts.
    B. The bookshelf Andrea dusts.
    C. Andrea dusts the bookshelf.
    D. Dusts the bookshelf Andrea.

14. A. Terry the bookshelf builds.
    B. Builds Terry the bookshelf.
    C. Terry builds the bookshelf.
    D. The bookshelf builds Terry.

15. A. Carrie a cupcake eats.
    B. A cupcake eats Carrie.
    C. Carrie eats a cupcake.
    D. Eats Carrie a cupcake.

16. A. Buys Henry eggs.
    B. Henry eggs buys.
    C. Eggs buys Henry.
    D. Henry buys eggs.

17 A. Gwen hamburgers barbecues.
    B. Gwen barbecues hamburgers.
    C. Barbecues Gwen hamburgers.
    D. Hamburgers barbecues Gwen.

18. A. Jill answers the door.
    B. The door answers Jill.
    C. Jill the door answers.
    D. Answers Jill the door.

19. A. Writes Stella a letter.
    B. Writes a letter Stella.
    C. Stella a letter writes.
    D. Stella writes a letter.

20. A. Jessie dusts the table.
    B. Jessie the table dusts.
    C. The table dusts Jessie.
    D. Dusts Jessie the table.

21. A. Henry washes the car.
    B. The car Henry washes.
    C. Henry the car washes.
    D. Washes the car Henry.

22. A. Carrie some carrots steams.
    B. Carrie carrots some steams.
    C. Carrie steams some carrots.
    D. Some carrots Carrie steams.

23. A. A movie watches Mike.
    B. Mike a movie watches.
    C. A movie Mike watches.
    D. Mike watches a movie.

24. A. Todd the house builds.
    B. Todd builds the house.
    C. The house Todd builds.
    D. Builds Todd the house.

25. A. Henry has a hat.
    B. Henry a hat has.
    C. A hat Henry has.
    D. Has Henry a hat.

Forming the Plural. When the noun is singular, use the base form. When the noun is plural, add "s" to the ending of regular nouns.

Singular	Plural
one (1) bathtub	two (2) bathtubs
one cake	three (3) cakes
one door	four (4) doors
one egg	five (5) eggs
one floor	six (6) floors
one hamburger	seven (7) hamburgers
one letter	eight (8) letters
one newspaper	nine (9) newspapers
one phone	ten (10) phones

The numbers in English are written out above: "one" = "1"; "two" = "2"; and so on. Practice saying the numbers.

Speaking Exercises. For each of the verb phrases listed below, say a person's name and then complete the sentence with the verb phrase. Practice saying the phrases as a class, and then call upon students individually.

✓ Verb Phrases

1. bakes a cake
   bakes a casserole
   bakes a quiche

2. barbecues chicken
   barbecues pork
   barbecues steaks

3. boils eggs
   boils potatoes
   boils rice

4. cooks dinner
   cooks a ham
   cooks a steak

5. steams the broccoli
   steams vegetables
   steams the milk

➾ Practice the groups of phrases above. Repeat adding one of the phrases below to each of the sentences.

A. on the stove
B. on the grill
C. in the oven
D. in the microwave

✓ Verb Phrases

1. cuts the cake
   cuts the steak
   cuts the potatoes

2. eats breakfast
   eats dinner
   eats the food

3. serves breakfast
   serves dinner
   serves the meal

4. feeds the dog
   feeds the ducks
   feeds the gold fish

5. reads a book
   reads a letter
   reads a newspaper

6. write an e-mail
   writes an essay
   writes a letter

➾ Practice the phrases above. Repeat adding one of the phrases below to each:

A. in the chair
B. on the couch
C. on the bed
D. at the desk
E. at the dinner table
F. on the coffee table
G. on the nightstand

Verb Phrases

1. plays a CD
   plays a DVD
   plays video games

2. talks on the phone
   talks to her friend
   talks with his sister

3. dusts the bookshelf
   dusts the table
   dusts the TV

4. scrubs the bathtub
   scrubs the sink
   scrubs the toilet

5. answers the phone
   answers the door
   answers the question

6. calls a friend
   calls his mother
   calls her father

7. vacuums the drapes
   vacuums the floor
   vacuums the furniture

➾ Practice saying the verb phrases above. Repeat adding the room where it happens:

A. in the kitchen
B. in the living room
C. in the dining room
D. in the bedroom
E. in the bathroom
F. in the closet
G. in the garage

Exercise 1.2

Sentence Building. Write the words in the subject-verb-object order to form sentences. Make sure the first letter of each sentence is capitalized, and the sentence ends in a period.

1. Mike / the door / answers

   ____

2. Stella / a quiche / bakes

   ____

3. Todd / a chicken / barbecues

   ____

4. the woman / potatoes / boils

   ____

5. the man / the toast / burns

____

6. Carrie / a friend / calls

____

7. Tim / a letter / reads

____

8. Julie / the table / dusts

____

9. Jill / the toast / eats

____

10. Billy / the dog / feeds

____

11. Andrea / a video game / plays

____

12. scrubs / Kim / the sink

____

13. Phil / the meal / serves

____

14. Darryl / the table / sets

____

15. Jennifer / cereal and toast / eats

____

16. Mike / the vegetables / steams

____

17. Emma / a letter / writes

____

18. John / noodles / boils

____

19. Susan / on the phone / talks

____

20. Dave / a stew / cooks

____

➾ Practice saying the sentences.

✐ **Writing.** Learn the vocabulary below and write a few sentences describing things your family members eat in your house. Share the sentences in your group.

Breakfast is usually eaten in the morning; lunch around noon; and dinner in the evening. English-speaking people usually eat different foods at different times of day. Dinner may be followed with a dessert.

✐ Breakfast

toast
eggs
bacon
hashbrowns
cereal

✐ Lunch

sandwich
soup
salad
hamburger
french fries

✐ Dinner

chicken
steak
ham
fish
casserole

✐ Dessert

cake
cupcake
pie
pastry
ice cream

✐ Drinks	Verbs: Cooking	Eating and Drinking
water	bake / s	drink / s
coffee	barbecue / s	eat / s
wine	boil / s	have / has
milk	cook / s	tea
	fry / ies	
	make / s	
	steam / s	
	toast / s	

*Add “s” to the third person singular form.

➾ Check your sentences for word order and word form.

CHAPTER 2: In the Park

Grammar

English is a subject-verb-object language. The subject can be singular (one subject) or plural (two or more subjects). The verb must agree with its subject. The verbs in this chapter are in the present tense. The present tense is used to mean that the action happens now, or that the action happens regularly. So, "John feeds the ducks" can mean he feeds them now, or he feeds them every weekend.

Dialogue

Dialogue for pronunciation and intonation. The teacher reads to the class, emphasizing pronunciation and intonation. The teacher reads Henry's part while students read Dave's part. Students pair up and practice the dialogue, and then switch parts and practice again. The teacher corrects pronunciation and intonation.

Henry Who is in the park today?
Dave John is in the park.
Henry What does he do there?
Dave He feeds the ducks.
Henry Who else is in the park?
Dave Mike and Sang-hee.
Henry What do they do in the park?
Dave Mike throws a ball for his dog, and Sang-hee runs in the park.
Henry What else happens at the park?
Dave Joong is getting married.
Henry That's great! Were you invited?
Dave Yes, he's my cousin.
Henry Is he marrying the woman he took to the New Year's Eve party?
Dave Yes, he's marrying Stella.
Henry You don't sound too happy about that.
Dave I'm happy for Joong.
Henry Uh-oh. What's wrong?
Dave She used to be my girlfriend.

Vocabulary

✐ Nouns

- ball
- cousin
- dog
- duck
- girlfriend
- New Year's Eve
- park
- party
- today
- woman

✐ Verbs

- do
- feed
- get married
- happen
- invite
- run
- sound
- throw
- took
- used to
- were

Exercise 2.1

Underline the subject and circle the verb in the sentences below.

1. John takes bread to the park.

2. John feeds the ducks.

3. Mike and Sang-hee walk their dogs to the park.

4. Mike plays with his dog.

5. He throws a ball.

6. The dog catches the ball and returns it.

7. Sang-hee and her dog run in the park.

8. The wedding is in the park today.

9. John likes the wedding music.

10. The ducks do not like the music.

11. One duck flies away.

12. The ducks fly away.

13. Sang-hee runs around the park.

14. Mike points to Sang-hee.

15. Mike's dog barks and wags his tail.

16. Sang-hee comes to them.

17. Mike and Sang-hee go home.

18. John goes home.

19. John walks to the park.

20. Sang-hee feeds the dog.

21. Stella pets the dog.

22. The dog comes to Stella.

23. The party is fun.

24. The bride is beautiful.

25. The groom is handsome.

➾ Practice saying the sentences.

Regular Verbs. Regular verbs change form for a third person singular subject. An "s" is added to the base form.

1st pers. sing.	I cook	*1st pers. pl.*	we cook
2nd pers. sing.	you cook	*2nd pers. pl.*	you cook
3rd pers. sing.	he / she cooks	*3rd pers. pl.*	they cook

Base	3rd person singular	pronunciation
bark	barks	/ s /
come	comes	/ z /
eat	eats	/ s /
feed	feeds	/ z /
like	likes	/ s /
play	plays	/ z /
point	points	/ s /
run	runs	/ z /
sound	sounds	/ z /
throw	throws	/ z /
wag	wags	/ z /
walk	walks	/ s /

Speaking. The "s" changes the pronunciation of the verbs. For "likes" and "walks," the "s" is pronounced / s /, the unvoiced sybilant; however, the "s" in "plays" and "wags" is pronounced / z /, the voiced sybilant. The "s" is unvoiced (/ s /) when it follows unvoiced consonants like / t /. The "s" is voiced (/ z /) when it follows voiced consonants like / d / and vowels. Practice saying the words above.

Excercise 2.2

Circle the correct form. Decide whether the subject of each sentence below is singular or plural. Then circle the correct verb form for each.

1. John and Mike walk / walks to the park.
2. Sang-hee run / runs in the park.
3. Dave and Henry like / likes Stella.
4. Joong cook / cooks a steak.
5. Two dogs wag / wags their tails.
6. One dog bark / barks at Stella.
7. Todd point / points at the dog.

8. Six ducks play / plays in the water.

9. Joong sound / sounds happy.

10. The ducks eat / eats the bread.

11. Sang-hee and Mike feed / feeds the dogs.

12. Sang-hee throw / throws a ball.

13. John and Mike come / comes home.

14. Sang-hee and Mike barbecue / barbecues chicken.

15. John bake / bakes a cake.

16. Susan point / points at the ducks.

17. Mike eat / eats a steak.

18. Carrie like / likes cupcakes.

19. Susan feed / feeds the chickens.

20. John and Henry feed / feeds the chickens.

21. Emma and Susan rollerblade / rollerblades in the park.

22. Mike and Henry play / plays basketball in the park.

23. Mike play / plays basketball in the park.

24. John listen / listens to music.

25. Dave and Joong listen / listens to music.

Exercise 2.3

Matching. Write the correct letter (A, B, C, or D) in the blanks below. Use each letter at least once. The letters can be used more than once. For most verb phrases, only one answer is correct.

1. _____ runs in the park.
2. _____ run in the park.
3. _____ play in the park.
4. _____ plays in the park.
5. _____ cook a steak.
6. _____ cooks a steak.
7. _____ teach English.
8. _____ teaches English.

A. Sang-hee and Mike
B. The man
C. The dog
D. The ducks

For some English verbs, "es" is added to the base of the verb to form the third person singular form.

Base	3rd person singular	Pronunciation
catch	catches	/ əz /
latch	latches	/ əz /
preach	preaches	/ əz /
scratch	scratches	/ əz /
teach	teaches	/ əz /
do	does	/ duz /
go	goes	/ gōz /

Speaking. When "es" follows "ch," it is pronounced as another syllable that includes a short vowel sound with / z / at the end. When the "es" follows "o," there is no extra syllable, and the "e" is not pronounced. Practice saying the words.

Irregular verb paradigms.

For "es" verbs, it is still only the third person singular that differs from the rest.

1st pers. sing.	I catch	*1st pers. pl.*	we catch
2nd pers. sing.	you catch	*2nd pers. pl.*	you catch
3rd pers. sing.	he / she catches	*3rd pers. pl.*	they catch

1st pers. sing.	I do	*1st pers. pl.*	we do
2nd pers. sing.	you do	*2nd pers. pl.*	you do
3rd pers. sing.	he / she does	*3rd pers. pl.*	they do

Comeplete the present tense paradigm for "go"

1st pers. sing.	I _______	*1st pers. pl.*	we ______
2nd pers. sing.	you ______	*2nd pers. pl.*	you ______
3rd pers. sing.	she ______	*3rd pers. pl.*	they ______

Exercise 2.4

Fill in: Write the correct form of the present tense verb in the blanks below.

1. The dog ________ the ball.
   (catch)

2 . Mike and John ________ the dog to catch the ball.
   (teach)

3. Mike ________ the dog to catch the ball.
   (teach)

4. The dogs _________ the ball.
   (catch)

5. Sang-hee ______ to the park.
   (go)

6 John and Mike _______ their homework.
   (do)

7. John ______ his homework.
   (do)

8. Sang-hee and Sarah _____ to the park.
(go)

9. Sarah _______ the door.
(latch)

10. Sarah and Tim ________ the door.
(latch)

11. The dog ________ his ear.
(scratch)

12. Two dogs ________ their ears.
(scratch)

13. Nathan ________ in the church.
(preach)

14. Nathan and Daniel ________ in the church.
(preach)

15. Mike ________ English.
(teach)

16. Sang-hee and Mike ________ English.
(teach)

17. Emma _________ Henry's back.
(scratch)

18. Terry __________ a TV show.
(watch)

19. Andrea and Terry ________ a TV show.
(watch)

20. Jill and Andrea ________ a movie.
(watch)

➾ Practice saying the sentences.

Another type of irregular verb ends in a consonant followed by "y." The third person singular is formed by changing "y" to "i" and adding "es."

Base	3rd person sing.	Pronunciation
cry	cries	/ īz /
fly	flies	/ īz /
try	tries	/ īz /

1st pers. sing.	I fly	*1st pers. pl.*	we fly
2nd pers. sing.	you fly	*2nd pers. pl.*	you fly
3rd pers. sing.	he / she flies	*3rd pers. pl.*	they fly

1st pers. sing.	I try	*1st pers. pl.*	we try
2nd pers. sing.	you try	*2nd pers. pl.*	you try
3rd pers. sing.	he / she tries	*3rd pers. pl.*	they try

Complete the present tense paradigm for "cry" below.

1st pers. sing.	I _______	*1st pers. pl.*	we _________
2nd pers. sing.	you _______	*2nd pers. pl.*	you ________
3rd pers. sing.	he ______	*3rd pers. pl.*	they ________

Practice saying the paradigm.

To Be: The "be" verb is irregular in most languages. This is a linking verb because it links the subject to an adjective that describes the subject: for example, "I am tired," "He is tall," and "She is smart." "Tired," "tall," and "smart" are adjectives; they describe the subjects of the sentences.

1st pers. sing.	I am	*1st pers. pl.*	we are
2nd pers. sing.	you are	*2nd pers. pl.*	you are
3rd pers. sing.	he / she / it is	*3rd pers. pl.*	they are

Practice saying the paradigm.

EXERCISE 2.5

Fill in: Write the correct form of the present tense "be" verb in the blanks below.

1. The man ________ tall.
2. We ________ tall.
3. The dogs ________ old.
4. She ________ old.
5. The woman ________ smart.
6. You ________ smart.
7. The girls ________ nice.
8. I ________ nice.
9. The boy ________ smart.
10. I ________ happy.
11. They ________ happy.
12. The car ________ black.
13. The houses ________ pink.
14. The exercise ________ easy.
15. The teacher ________ hard.
16. You ________ hard.
17. The house ________ on the corner.
18. We ________ in the park.
19. I ________ on the corner.
20. I ________ in the park.

➾ Practice saying the sentences.

🔍 **To Have** is also irregular.

1st pers. sing.	I have	*1st pers. pl.*	we have
2nd pers. sing.	you have	*2nd pers. pl.*	you have
3rd pers. sing.	he / she / it has	*3rd pers. pl.*	they have

➾ Practice saying the paradigm.

EXERCISE 2.6

Fill in: Write the correct form of the present tense "have" verb in the blanks below.

1. I _________ a house.
2. He _________ dogs.
3. They _________ a bike.
4. You _________ a wedding.
5. We _________ a car.
6. They _________ ducks.
7. I _________ a cup of coffee.
8. You _________ a slice of toast.
9. They _________ bacon and eggs.
10. We _________ a picnic.
11. She _________ a steak.
12. We _________ two TVs.
13. I _________ a dog.
14. She _________ a phone call.
15. It _________ a door.

➾ Practice saying the sentences.

Speaking: Things We Do in the Park. For each of the verb phrases listed below, say a person's name and complete the sentence with the verb phrase. Practice saying the list with a partner.

✓ Verb Phrases

walk the dog	train the dog
run	look at the trees and plants
bike	see the tea garden
rollerblade	take pictures
skateboard	sit in the tea garden
play frisbee	sit in the sunshine
play baseball	listen to music
play basketball	have a wedding
play on the bars	have a picnic
swing on the swing	have a private conversation
slide down the slide	feed the ducks
climb the rock wall	row a boat

PREPOSITIONS: on, down, at, in, to

Exercise 2.7

Fill in: Write the correct form of the present tense verbs in the blanks below.

1. The woman ________ the dog.
(walk)

2. The man _________ at the trees.
(look)

3. John and Dave _______ pictures.
(take)

4. Sang-hee ______ the tea garden.
(see)

5. Joong _____ in the sunshine.
(sit)

6. Mike and Sang-hee _____ in the tea garden.
(sit)

7. John _______ to music.
(listen)

8. Stella ______ at her wedding.
(cry)

9. Tim and Todd ________ basketball.
(play)

10. Carrie and Sarah ______________ in the park.
(rollerblade)

11. Carrie _____________ around the park.
(rollerblade)

12. The man ______ frisbee.
(play)

13. The woman ________ on the swing.
(swing)

14. The child _______ down the slide.
(slide)

15. The child _______ the dog.
(train)

16. Jill ________ the rock wall.
(climb)

17. Andrea and Jill _________ the rock wall.
(climb)

18. Joong and Stella ______ in the park.
(bike)

19. Joong ______ in the park.
(bike)

20. Joong and Stella _______ a private conversation.
(have)

21. Susan ____________ in the park.
(skateboard)

22. Susan and Kim ____________ in the park.
(skateboard)

23. Carrie and Susan ______ a boat.
(row)

24. Susan ______ a boat.
(row)

25. Mike ______ pictures.
(take)

Writing. Write a few present tense sentences describing things you do or see in a park. Share the sentences in your group.

Take home writing assignment. Draw a picture of a person or people doing something in a park. Or, cut one out of a magazine or print one from the Internet. Write several sentences in which you describe what is happening in the picture. Answer such questions as the following, though not necessarily in this order.

- Where are the people, or what is the name of the place in the picture?
- Who or what is in the center of the picture? What is that person or thing doing?
- Who or what is above center in the picture? What is that person or thing doing?
- Who or what is in the upper left corner? What is that person or thing doing?
- Who or what is in the upper right corner? What is that person or thing doing?
- Who or what is below the center of the picture? What is that person or thing doing?
- Who or what is in the lower left corner? What is that person or thing doing?
- Who or what is in the lower right corner? What is that person or thing doing?

Check your sentences for word order and word form.

Read the paragraph below and draw a picture of what you see.

Friends have a picnic on the grass in the park. The sun is shining, and the sky is blue. There are many green trees in the park. Emma brings fried chicken. Henry brings potato salad. John and Sang-hee bring a cake. Mike brings iced tea. Susan barbecues corn on the cob. They talk together and eat lunch. The company is charming. The food is delicious. They are happy.

Paragraph form. The first line of the paragraph above is indented. Each sentence begins with a capital letter and ends with a period. There is one space between words and after punctuation marks. Each line is filled from beginning to end, regardless of where the sentences end. This is paragraph form.

Rewrite your sentences into a paragraph like the one above.

Chapter 3: In the Yard

Grammar

Past tense, regular and irregular verbs. Most of the verbs in this chapter are past tense verbs. Since the past tense is natural to English, no extra words are necessary to form the past tense. The regular way to form the past tense is to add "ed" to the ending.

Dialogue

Dialogue for pronunciation and intonation. The teacher reads to the class, emphasizing pronunciation and intonation. The teacher reads Sally's part while students read Todd's part. Students pair up and practice the dialogue, and then switch parts and practice again. The teacher corrects pronunciation and intonation.

Sally	Hi, Todd. I didn't know you lived here. What did you do with your yard?
Todd	Hi, Sally. I'm glad you came over. I moved into this house five years ago. I worked on my yard this weekend. Watch your step. Walk on the concrete. I just watered the yard. It's very muddy. I took out old plants and planted new plants.
Sally	What happened to your redwood trees?
Todd	I removed my redwood trees. They were too tall. A storm might knock them over.
Sally	That's too bad. I liked them. But they touched the power lines, didn't they?
Todd	Yes, they were too tall.
Sally	A storm knocked Mike's redwood tree down on his house last year. Repairs were expensive.
Todd	It was too tall.
Sally	It was too tall. What else did you do in your yard?
Todd	I planted rose bushes. I mowed the lawn. I fertilized the camellias. I picked peaches and zucchini. I ate a peach this morning, and it was sweet. I gave some to Henry. Here, let me get you a bag. You can take some home for your family.
Sally	I see. You have been working hard. Everything looks so nice. And thank you. I'd love to take some peaches and zucchini home, but not too many. I have no one to share them with. My husband died last year.

Todd	I'm sorry. I didn't know. So, tell me, what have you been doing with your yard?
Sally	Oh, same as ever. I picked the seeds from the sunflowers in fall and planted them in spring. I wired little junipers to make bonsai for the shop.
Todd	What kind of shop?
Sally	I started a craft store. I have a partner: my sister Shirley. She's a bit younger. She works the cash register and does the cleaning. I do everything else.
Todd	Wow, that's really interesting.

Vocabulary

✓ Past Tense Verbs

ate
came
did
didn't
died
fertilized
gave
happened
knocked
liked
lived
moved

mowed
picked
planted
removed
started
took
touched
was
watered
were
wired
worked

✓ Present tense verbs

let

✓ Nouns

bag
bonsai
camellia
cash register
cleaning
concrete
craft store

fall
hedge
home
husband
juniper
last year
lawn

partner
peach
plants
power line
redwood tree
repairs
rose bush
seeds
shop
spring
step
storm
sunflower
weekend
yard
years
zucchini

✐ Adjectives

interesting
muddy
new
old
same
some
too bad
too tall
younger

✐ Indefinite Pronouns

everything
no one

A. Forms of Regular Verbs. The past tense form is the same for all persons.

Base	Past tense (+ "-ed")	Pronunciation
work	worked	/ t /
water	watered	/ d /
plant	planted	/ əd /
happen	happened	/ d /
touch	touched	/ t /
mow	mowed	/ d /
pick	picked	/ t /
start	started	/ əd /

All regular past tense verbs end in / t / or / d /. When the base form of the verb ends in / t / or / d /, another syllable / əd / is pronounced. When the base ends in a unvoiced sound, the end sound is / t /; when the base ends in a voiced or vowel sound, the end sound is / d /. Practice saying the words.

Exercise 3.1

Rewrite the sentences below to make them past tense.

1. Henry works in his yard.

   ____

2. Sang-hee waters the rose bushes.

   ____

3. Sally plants junipers.

   ____

4. Todd touches the tree.

   ____

5. Mike mows the lawn.

   ____

6. The accident happens today.

   ____

7. Susan picks a peach.

   ____

8. Sang-hee starts the lawn mower.

   ____

9. Emma greets the man.

   ____

10. The man lifts the box.

    ____

11. Sally and Shirley work at the store.

    ____

12. We mow the lawn.

    ____

13. You pick the flowers.

____

14. The dog touches my hand.

____

15. The farmers plant rice.

____

16. The workers water the park trees.

____

17. We work every day.

____

18. He walks to school.

____

19. Emma boils an egg.

____

20. Sang-hee and Mike cook dinner.

____

21. Henry and Tim dust the bookshelves.

____

22. Kim answers the question.

____

23. You steam some vegetables.

____

24. Todd vacuums the floor.

____

25. We toast the bread.

____

➾ Practice saying the sentences.

B. Very irregular and very often used verbs. English has hundreds of irregular verbs, all of them originating in Old English. The irregular verbs must be memorized.

Present tense	Past tense
I am / he is	I / he was
you / we / they are	you / we / they were
do	did
go	went
have	had

➾ Practice saying the verbs in the present and past tenses.

Most of these irregular verbs have changed little from the Old English. Exceptionally, Modern English "went" comes from the Old English "wendan" > Middle English "wend," while "go" comes directly from the Old English "gengan."

Exercise 3.2

Multiple Choice. Circle the letter in front of the correct past tense sentence for each of the groups of sentences below.

1. A. I goed home.
   B. I wented home.
   C. I went home.
   D. I is home.

2. A. I doed the work.
   B. I ded the work.
   C. I done the work.
   D. I did the work.

3. A. They was happy.
   B. They were happy.
   C. They is happy.
   D. They are happy.

4 A. They went to the store.
B. They goes to the store.
C. They goed to the store.
D. They is to the store.

5. A. Susan did her homework.
B. Susan dod her homework.
C. Susan do her homework.
D. Susan ded her homework.

6. A. We go to school.
B. We went to school.
C. We goed to school.
D. We god to school.

7. A. Mike hased a dog.
B. Mike haved a dog.
C. Mike had a dog.
D. Mike hadded a dog.

8. A. She goes to the park.
B. She wented to the park.
C. She goed to the park.
D. She went to the park.

9. A. He was tall.
B. He were tall.
C. He are tall.
D. He am tall.

10. A. John had a cake.
B. John hasd a cake.
C. John hased a cake.
D. John haved a cake.

11. A. I am sad.
B. I were sad.
C. I was sad.
D. I is sad.

12. A. Sally and Todd had a big yard.
B. Sally and Todd haved a big yard.
C. Sally and Todd hadded a big yard.
D. Sally and Todd hased a big yard.

13. A. We done it.
    B. We dod it.
    C. We ded it.
    D. We did it.

14. A. We were glad.
    B. We was glad.
    C. We is glad.
    D. We am glad.

15. A. Emma hased a house.
    B. Emma haved a house.
    C. Emma had a house.
    D. Emma has a house.

16. A. You was smart.
    B. You were smart.
    C. You am smart.
    D. You is smart.

17. A. You goed to the beach.
    B. You goes to the beach.
    C. You went to the beach.
    D. You wended to the beach.

18. A. Tim haved good grades.
    B. Tim has good grades.
    C. Tim hased good grades.
    D. Tim had good grades.

19. A. Sang-hee and Mike did lunch.
    B. Sang-hee and Mike done lunch.
    C. Sang-hee and Mike doed lunch.
    D. Sang-hee and Mike dod lunch.

20. A. Henry had a bird.
    B. Henry has a bird.
    C. Henry haved a bird.
    D. Henry hast a bird.

21. A. He liked the TV show.
    B. He likes the TV show.
    C. He likened the TV show.
    D. He like the TV show.

22. A. They tryed the bacon and eggs.
    B. They tries the bacon and eggs.
    C. They tried the bacon and eggs.
    D. They try the bacon and eggs.

23. A. We was in the park.
    B. We were in the park.
    C. We wased in the park.
    D. We is in the park.

24. A. I ised on the phone.
    B. I am on the phone.
    C. I were on the phone.
    D. I was on the phone.

25. A. You hased a good dinner.
    B. You has a good dinner.
    C. You have a good dinner.
    D. You had a good dinner.

Exercise 3.3

Fill in. Fill in the blank with the past tense form of the verb.

1. Emma and Susan _____ to the park.
   (go)

2. The man ______ a party.
   (has)

3. John _____ a tall man.
   (is)

4. Andrea and Jill _____ the job.
   (do)

5. We ______ happy.
   (are)

6. We _______ a big house.
   (have)

7. He ______ to Europe last year.
(go)

8. Todd _____ the best job.
(do)

9. They _______ college students.
(are)

10. Todd and Sally ______ to the temple.
(go)

11. Todd and Sally _________ steak for dinner.
(have)

12. Todd ______ not know Jason died.
(do)

13. Kim and Tim ______ twins.
(are)

14. Tim _______ a nice car.
(has)

15. Emma and Henry _______ Dominican.
(are)

16. Emma _______ a purple hat.
(has)

17. I _______ to the beach.
(go)

18. I ______ my homework.
(do)

19. I _____ so happy.
(am)

20. I ________ a lot of money.
(have)

21. You ______ a child.
(are)

22. You ______ to the beach.
(go)

23. Dave ______ a cousin named Joong.
(has)

24. Dave ______ the laundry.
(does)

25. The man ____ sad.
(is)

26. The man ______ to Brazil last summer.
(goes)

26. Henry ______ a sister named Susan.
(has)

27. Sally _______ not know Todd lived there.
(does)

28. I ______ a good student.
(am)

29. They ______ good students.
(are)

30. English ______ many irregular verbs.
(has)

31. You ______ your English homework.
(do)

32. English _____ fun.
(is)

➾ Practice saying the sentences above.

Irregular Verbs that Change the Vowel Sound in the Base Form. No ending is added. Most irregular verbs are of this type. These irregular verbs come from Old English and are used often in Modern English. They are called strong verbs because of the vowel change.

C. Vowel Changes to A

Present tense	Past tense
begin	began
come	came
drink	drank
eat	ate
give	gave
run	ran
see	saw
sit	sat

Practice saying the present and past tense forms.

Exercise 3.4

Multiple choice. Circle the letter in front of the sentence with the correct form of the past tense verb.

1. A. I seed him on the roof.
   B. I saw him on the roof.
   C. I seen him on the roof.
   D. I sawed him on the roof.

2. A. The woman sat on the bench.
   B. The woman satted on the bench.
   C. The woman sitted on the bench.
   D. The woman setted on the bench.

3. A. I eated at the restaurant.
   B. I ate at the restaurant.
   C. I ated at the restaurant.
   D. I eaten at the restaurant.

4. A. John runned to the park.
   B. John rund to the park.
   C. John ran to the park.
   D. John ranned to the park.

5. A. They gived money to the poor.
   B. They gave money to the poor.
   C. They gived money to the poor.
   D. They given money to the poor.

6. A. We comed to the store.
   B. We come to the store.
   C. We camed to the store.
   D. We came to the store.

7. A. You drinked the coffee.
   B. You drunk the coffee.
   C. You drunked the coffee.
   D. You drank the coffee.

8. A. They sawed the ocean.
   B. They saw the ocean.
   C. They seen the ocean.
   D. They sead the ocean.

9. A. You camed home.
   B. You comed home.
   C. You came home.
   D. You camen home.

10. A. The woman gave him a TV.
    B. The woman gived him a TV.
    C. The woman given him a TV.
    D. The woman gaved him a TV.

11. A. The teacher begun the lesson.
    B. The teacher beginned the lesson.
    C. The teacher began the lesson.
    D. The teacher begint the lesson.

12. A. The dog runned after the ducks.
    B. The dog raned after the ducks.
    C. The dog ranned after the ducks.
    D. The dog ran after the ducks.

13. A. We sitted in the classroom.
    B. We set in the classroom.
    C. We satted in the classroom.
    D. We sat in the classroom.

14. A. The seed becomes a tree.
    B. The seed becomed a tree.
    C. The seed became a tree.
    D. The seed become a tree.

15. A. You forgives them.
    B. You forgive them.
    C. You forgived them.
    D. You forgave them.

16. A. I swam in the ocean.
    B. I swimmed in the ocean.
    C. I swim in the ocean.
    D. I swims in the ocean.

Exercise 3.5

Fill in. For each of the sentences below, fill in the blank with the correct past tense form of the verb.

1. The movie ________.
   (begin)

2. Todd ______ pie.
   (eat)

3. Sally ________ a dog.
   (see)

4. Sang-hee and Mike ______ in the sunshine.
   (sit)

5. Henry _______ the dog a treat.
   (give)

6. Sang-hee _______ in the park.
   (run)

7. Andrea and Jill _______ coffee.
   (drink)

8. The wedding _________ on time.
   (begin)

9. They ______ dinner.
(eat)

10. We ________ to the party.
(come)

11. You _______ the rose bushes.
(see)

12. You ______ what they did.
(see)

13. You _______ chocolates to your friends.
(give)

14. I ________ too much coffee.
(drink)

15. The choir _______ to sing.
(begin)

16. Henry _________ hungry.
(become)

17. The teacher _________ the late student.
(forgive)

18. Todd _________ to the shore.
(swim)

19. Darryl ________ tired.
(become)

20. The students ________ the late teacher.
(forgive)

21. The dog _________ across the lake.
(swim)

22. Carrie and Susan ______ the broccoli.
(eat)

23. You _______ the new red car.
(see)

24. The student ____ in the desk.
(sit)

25. John _______ Dave a job.
(give)

➾ Practice saying the sentences aloud.

Speaking Excercise. For each of the verb phrases listed below, say a person's name, or two people's names as needed, and then complete the sentence with the past tense verb phrase. Practice saying the list with a partner.

Past Tense Verb Phrases

1. ate the bread
   ate the peach
   ate the zuccini

2. began a business
   began her homework
   began school

3. came to school
   came to work
   came to the store

4. did his homework
   did the cleaning
   didn't do his homework
   didn't do the cleaning

5. drank water
   drank coffee
   drank tea

6. gave the peach to Sally
   gave a flower to Sang-hee
   gave money to the child

7. had an accident
   had a peach tree
   had a question

8. liked school
   liked English
   liked trees

9. lived in the house
   lived near school
   lived in America

10. moved into the house
    moved to New York
    moved to London

11. planted the tree
    planted the bush
    planted the flower

12. ran in the park
    ran to the campus
    ran a business

13. sat in the chair
    sat in the tea garden
    sat on the bed

14. saw the redwood tree
    saw the beach
    saw the storm

15. talked on the phone
    talked to his friend
    talked to her brother

16. took the plants
    took the boxes
    took the bag

17. wanted the bread
    wanted the flower
    wanted the flower

18. was too tall
    was interesting
    was interested in plants

19. went to the house
    went to the campus
    went home

20. were interesting
    were interested in English
    were interested in trees

21. worked on campus
    worked at home
    worked the cash register

Reading: The Landscaping Business.

Twenty years ago, Sarah and Sally began a business together. They were landscapers at the University of Central California. They liked working outdoors. They worked hard. They planted trees, bushes, and flowers. They came to campus every day. They watered, fertilized, and trimmed the plants. They ate lunch on campus and talked about their work. They saw the campus change from empty squares of concrete into a lush garden. When old plants died, they removed them and replaced them with new plants. They did everything themselves.

Last year, Sally and Sarah decided they were too old to lift and carry heavy plants and tools. Sally retired, and Sarah hired Kim and Tim as assistants. Sarah ran the business, and Kim and Tim cared for the plants. They happened to live nearby, and they loved working outdoors. They learned a lot about plants from Sarah. They were also students at the university. They had biology class together. Tim wanted to become a botanist, and Kim wanted to become a science writer. They went to their professor Dr. Jones to ask about getting into graduate school, and she gave them advice. They asked Sarah to write them a letter of recommendation, and they were accepted.

Vocabulary

Verbs

accepted	hired
become	learned
cared	lift
carry	loved
change	recommend
decided	replace

retired
talked
trimmed

Nouns

advice
assistants
biology
botanists
business
campus
class
college
flowers
landscapers
professor
school
tools

Adjectives

a lot
empty
graduate
hard
heavy
interested
lush
square
together

Comprehension Activity: Multiple Choice.

1. Where did Sarah and Sally work?

   A. They worked in the park.
   B. They worked in the house.
   C. They worked on campus.
   D. They worked in the yard.

2. Why did Sarah and Sally want to be landscapers?

   A. They liked working outdoors.
   B. They liked working on campus.
   C. They liked working with plants.
   D. They liked working in the morning.

3. What did the campus change from?

   A. The campus changed from a lush garden.
   B. The campus changed from a muddy yard.
   C. The campus changed from a park.
   D. The campus changed from empty squares of concrete.

4. Why did Sally retire?

   A. Sally decided she liked working indoors.
   B. Sally decided she was too old to carry heavy plants.
   C. Sally decided to hire Kim and Tim.
   D. Sally decided to go to Brazil.

5. What did Kim and Tim do?

   A. Kim and Tim were landscapers.
   B. Kim and Tim were students at the university.
   C. Kim and Tim were botanists.
   D. Kim and Tim were professors.

6. What did Dr. Jones tell Kim and Tim?

   A. Dr. Jones told Kim and Tim to ask Sarah for a letter of recommendation for graduate school.
   B. Dr. Jones told Kim and Tim to go to graduate school.
   C. Dr. Jones told Kim and Tim not to go to graduate school.
   D. Dr. Jones told Kim and Tim to come to class on time.

Writing. Write a few sentences describing things you do in a yard or garden. Share the sentences in your group.

Take Home Writing Assignment. Draw a picture of a person or people working with plants. Or, cut one out of a magazine or print one from the Internet. Write a paragraph in which you describe what is happening in the picture. Answer such questions as the following, though not necessarily in this order.

- Where are the people, or what is the name of the place in the picture?
- Who or what is in the center of the picture? What is that person or thing doing?
- Who or what is above the center? What is that person or thing doing?
- Who or what is in the upper left corner? What is that person or thing doing?
- Who or what is in the upper right corner? What is that person or thing doing?
- Who or what is below the center? What is that person or thing doing?
- Who or what is in the lower left corner? What is that person or thing doing?
- Who or what is in the lower right corner? What is that person or thing doing?

Check your sentences for word order and word form.

Chapter 4: Going to the Mall

Grammar

Nouns, Personal Pronouns, Pronoun Cases, and Pronoun References.

Dialogue

Dialogue for pronunciation and intonation. The teacher reads to the class, emphasizing pronunciation and intonation. The teacher reads Henry's part while students read Emma's part. Students pair up and practice the dialogue, and then switch parts and practice again. The teacher corrects pronunciation and intonation.

Henry	Hi, Emma.
Emma	Hi, Henry. Did you find your book?
Henry	Yes, I found it. Are you writing an e-mail?
Emma	Yes, I'm writing it to Uncle Tomás.
Henry	Tell him I said hi.
Emma	OK.
Henry	Tell him we miss him. Are you going to the mall later?
Emma	OK. Yes, I need to buy shoes.
Henry	I'll drive you. I need to buy a hat and a pair of boots. Maybe we can get presents to send to him.
Emma	Thanks. We can get them together. Don't you also want to see someone?
Henry	Me? Who? I don't know what you mean.
Emma	You know.
Henry	I don't know who you're talking about.
Emma	Him.
Henry	Him who?
Emma	That manager.
Henry	And why do I need to see a manager?
Emma	The one at Macy's.
Henry	Well, I do need to go to Macy's to buy my hat and boots.
Emma	Of course you do. Me too. "Henry says hi, and he misses you. Love, Emma." I'm done. Let's go.
Henry	Do you remember their dog?

Emma	Uncle Tomás and Aunt Maria's dog? Sure.
Henry	How she used to steal my boots?
Emma	I remember she stole shoes. She took my favorite pair of high-heeled shoes.
Emma	And your boots?
Henry	Were eel-skin and much more expensive than your heels.
Emma	And always on the floor.
Henry	Let's go.
Emma	John is waiting.
Henry	That isn't funny.

Vocabulary

✐ Nouns

aunt
book
boots
e-mail
hat
high-heeled shoes
Macy's
mall
manager
pair
presents
shoes
uncle

✐ Pronouns

I*
me
them
you
your
it

*The pronoun "i" is capitalized.

✐ Verbs

buy
find
is waiting
is writing
left
let's (let us)
miss
need
remember
says
stole
used to

Nouns: Nouns are words that represent persons, places, things, or ideas.

Regular nouns: Regular nouns are made plural by adding "s" to the ending.

Singular	Plural	Pronunciation
one (1) book	eleven (11) books	/ s /
one e-mail	twelve (12) e-mails	/ z /
one uncle	thirteen (13) uncles	/ z /
one manager	fourteen (14) managers	/ z /
one shoe	fifteen (15) shoes	/ z /

Irregular nouns: "es" is added to the end of many English nouns.

Singular	Plural	Pronunciation
one box	sixteen (16) boxes	/ əz /
one bush	seventeen (17) bushes	/ əz /
one class	eighteen (18) classes	/ əz /
one couch	nineteen (19) couches	/ əz /
one glass	twenty (20) glasses	/ əz /
one potato	twenty-one (21) potatoes	/ tōz /

The "s" is unvoiced (/ s /) when it follows unvoiced consonants; the "s" is voiced (/ z /) when it follows voiced consonants and vowels. Practice saying the words.

Irregular nouns: English nouns ending in a consonant followed by "y" in the singular have to be changed to "ies" to form the plural.

Singular	Plural	Pronunciation
one berry / ē /	twenty-four berries	/ ēz /
one fry / ī /	twenty-five fries	/ īz /
one refectory / ē /	twenty-six refectories	/ ēz /
one supply / ī /	twenty-seven supplies	/ īz /

Exercise 4.1

Multiple Choice: Circle the letter in front of the sentence with the correct plural form of the noun(s).

1. A. Henry found the book.
   B. Henry found the books.
   C. Henry found the bookies.
   D. Henry found the bookes.

2. A. Emma wrote to her uncls.
   B. Emma wrote to her unclies.
   C. Emma wrote to her uncles.
   D. Emma wrote to her uncle.

3. A. John works in stors.
   B. John works in stores.
   C. John works in stories.
   D. John works in store.

4. A. Emma buys shoes.
   B. Emma buys shos.
   C. Emma buys shoies.
   D. Emma buys shoe.

5. A. John eats berrys.
   B. John eats berry.
   C. John eats berries.
   D. John eats berryes.

6. A. Todd waters the bushs.
   B. Todd waters the bushes.
   C. Todd waters the bushies.
   D. Todd waters the bush.

7. A. Sally lifts the boxs.
   B. Sally lifts the boxies.
   C. Sally lifts the box.
   D. Sally lifts the boxes.

8. A. The dog ran with the foxs.
   B. The dog ran with the foxies.
   C. The dog ran with the foxes.
   D. The dog ran with the foxys.

9. A. Tim likes his classs.
   B. Tim likes his classes.
   C. Tim likes his classies.
   D. Tim likes his class.

10. A. Mike moves couches.
    B. Mike moves couchies.
    C. Mike moves couchs.
    D. Mike moves couch.

11. A. Andrea boils potato.
    B. Andrea boils potatos.
    C. Andrea boils potatoes.
    D. Andrea boils potates.

12. A. Henry likes fries.
    B. Henry likes fryes.
    C. Henry likes fry.
    D. Henry likes frys.

13. A. Jill cut potatos to make frys.
    B. Jill cut potatoes to make fries.
    C. Jill cut potatoies to make fries.
    D. Jill cut potatoyes to make frys.

14. A. Tim took supplies.
    B. Tim took supply.
    C. Tim took supplys.
    D. Tim took supplyes.

15. A. Emma likes to go to mallies.
    B. Emma likes to go to malls.
    C. Emma likes to go to mallyes.
    D. Emma likes to go to mallys.

16. A. Henry wants to buy presenties.
    B. Henry wants to buy presentes.
    C. Henry wants to buy presents.
    D. Henry wants to buy presentys.

Exercise 4.2

Fill in. Write in the correct plural form of the noun.

1. Mike saw four _________ at Sally's house.
   (couch)

2. Sally lifted ________ on campus.
   (box)

3. Emma gave Henry some _________.
   (berry)

4. Henry ate _________.
   (cherry)

5. Emma had forty pairs of _________.
   (shoe)

6. Kim had six _______ at the college.
   (class)

7. Sang-hee washed the _______.
   (car)

8. Kim and Tim watered the _______.
   (plant)

9. Kim and Tim watered the _________.
   (bush)

10. Mike planted _________ in his yard.
    (potato)

11. Henry goes to _________ on weekends.
    (mall)

12. Emma and Henry have three _________.
    (uncle)

13. John made ____________ and ______ for lunch.
    (hamburger) (fry)

14. Tim took five _______ to school every day.
    (book)

15. Sally took _________ to Sarah.
(cherry)

16. The store had ____________ for sale.
(strawberry)

17. John bought __________ at the store.
(supply)

18. Tim and Kim studied ________ in biology.
(grass)

19. Sally filled ________ with tea.
(glass)

20. The ______ ran to the park.
(fox)

⇛ Practice saying the sentences.

Possesion. The possessive form of the noun is indicated with an apostrophe + "s" ('s) added to the ending.

Base	Possessive	Pronunciation
Henry	Henry's hat	/ rēz /
Uncle Tomás	Uncle Tomás's dog	/ əz /
manager	manager's desk	/ z /
student	student's homework	/ s /
landscaper	landscaper's tools	/ z /
dog	dog's ball	/ z /

When a plural noun is possessive, only the apostrophe (') is added to the ending.

Plural	Possessive	Pronunciation
Johnsons	Johnsons' house	/ z /
managers	managers' keys	/ z /
visitors	visitors' pass	/ z /
students	students' homework	/ s /

The "s" is unvoiced (/ s /) when it follows unvoiced consonants; the "s" is voiced (/ z /) when it follows voiced consonants and vowels. Practice saying the possessive forms above.

Personal Prounouns. Pronouns are words that stand in for nouns. Personal pronouns stand in for people.

Personal Pronouns

1st per. sing.	I	*1st per. pl.*	we
2nd per. sing.	you	*2nd per. pl.*	you
3rd per. sing.	he / she / it	*3rd per. pl.*	they
unspecified persons	who / whoever		

The "'s" at the end of possessive nouns like "Todd's house" is almost all that's left of the Old English case system. Old English nouns had endings that distinguished not only possessives but also objects from subjects. Pronouns still have the endings for the objective case.

✓ Pronoun Cases

As Subject	As Object	Possessive
I	me	my / mine
you	you	your
he	him	his (masculine gender)
she	her	her (feminine gender)
it	it	its
we	us	our
they	them	their
who	whom	whose
whoever	whomever	

Exercise 4.3

Multiple choice. Circle the letter in front of the sentence with correct possessive nouns and pronoun cases.

1. A. Me want the managers desk.
   B. Me want the manager's desk.
   C. I want the managers desk.
   D. I want the manager's desk.

2. A. We went to I house.
   B. We went to I's house.
   C. We went to my house.
   D. Us went to my house.

3. A. You like his dog.
   B. You like he dog.
   C. You like him dog.
   D. You like he's dog.

4. A. Emma bought she's shoes at Macy's.
   B. Emma bought her shoes at Macy's.
   C. Emma bought his shoes at Macy's.
   D. Emma bought she shoes at Macy's.

5. A. She drove he to the store.
   B. She drove his to the store.
   C. She drove him to the store.
   D. Her drove him to the store.

6. A. Them didn't know he.
   B. Them didn't know him.
   C. They didn't know he.
   D. They didn't know him.

7. A. Us found him at the mall.
   B. We found him at the mall.
   C. Us found his at the mall.
   D. We found he at the mall.

8. A. Henry ate Emma's steak.
   B. Henry's ate Emma steak.
   C. Henry's ate Emma's steak.
   D. Her ate him steak.

9. A. Who ate I steak?
   B. Whom ate my steak?
   C. Whose ate me steak?
   D. Who ate my steak?

10. A. Henry and John saw them.
    B. Henry and John saw their.
    C. Henry and John saw they.
    D. Henry and John saw they's.

11. A. The dog takes she.
    B. The dog takes its.
    C. The dog takes he.
    D. The dog takes it.

12. A. Uncle Tomás's dog took he.
    B. Uncle Tomás dog took it.
    C. Uncle Tomás's dog took it.
    D. Uncle Tomás' dog took they.

13. A. Emma buys her shoes at the mall.
    B. Emma buys she shoes at the mall.
    C. Emma buys she's shoes at the mall.
    D. Emma buys he shoes at the mall.

14. A. Him bought a hat for she.
    B. He bought a hat for her.
    C. He bought a hat for hem.
    D. His bought a hat for she.

15. A. She didn't know he name.
    B. She didn't know his name.
    C. Her didn't know he name.
    D. She didn't know him name.

16. A. Andrea wanted her books.
    B. Andrea wanted she books.
    C. Andrea wanted him books.
    D. Andrea wanted she's books.

17. A. Jill gave she's books to Andrea.
    B. Jill gave him books to Andrea.
    C. Jill gave her books to Andrea.
    D. Jill gave she books to Andrea.

18. A. They cook for her.
    B. Them cook for she.
    C. They cook for she.
    D. They cook for hers.

19. A. The dog had a steak in it mouth.
    B. The dog had a steak in it's mouth.
    C. The dog had a steak in him mouth.
    D. The dog had a steak in its mouth.

20. A. The manager sells we.
    B. The manager sells they.
    C. The manager sells their.
    D. The manager sells them.

21. A. The sales clerk sold me a pair of boots.
    B. The sales clerk sold he a pair of boots.
    C. The sales clerk sold she a pair of boots.
    D. The sales clerk sold I a pair of boots.

22. A. The Johnsons tea is sweet.
    B. The Johnson tea is sweet.
    C. The Johnsons' tea is sweet.
    D. The Johnson's tea is sweet.

23. A. Todd's yard is muddy.
    B. Todd yard is muddy.
    C. Todds yard is muddy.
    D. Todd's yard's is muddy.

24. A. They were glad to know we.
    B. They were glad to know us.
    C. Them were glad to know us.
    D. Them were glad to know we.

25. A. We didn't know the visitors.
    B. Us didn't know the visitors.
    C. We didn't know the visitors'.
    D. We didn't know the visitors's.

26. A. Us bought their house.
    B. We bought they house.
    C. We bought their house.
    D. We bought them house.

27. A. They saw they dog.
    B. They saw their dog.
    C. They saw them dog.
    D. Them saw their dog.

28. A. They house is on the corner.
    B. They's house is on the corner.
    C. Them house is on the corner.
    D. Their house is on the corner.

29. A. I didn't know your name.
    B. I didn't know you name.
    C. I didn't know youse name.
    D. Me didn't know your name.

30. A. You had your coat.
    B. Your had you coat.
    C. You had youse coat.
    D. You had you's coat.

Pronoun Antecedents. Personal pronouns refer to a person or persons who have already been mentioned. Pronouns require an "antecedent," a person or persons named earlier. For example, in the dialogue, when Henry says, "Yes, I found it," he is referring to the book Emma just asked about.

Exercise 4.4

Matching. For each sentence below, look for the antecedent and select the correct pronoun. Use each pronoun once. Not all pronouns will be used.

1. Tim helped Henry learn English. Later, Henry taught _______ French.

2. Henry wanted a hat. He bought _______ today.

3. We bought a house. _______ house is by the park.

4. Todd and I go to the park. _______ play football with them.

5. Mike and Sally moved the furniture. _______ did it themselves.

6. Todd found the bag of peaches. _______ bag is in the kitchen.

7. I bought clothes at the mall today. _______ like my new shoes.

8. Emma took the bus to the mall. _______ didn't have a car.

9. I saw Sang-hee walk _______ dog to the park.

10. He likes me. He sent flowers to _______ house.

A. I	G. him	M. we
B. me	H. his	N. us
C. my	I. she	O. our
D. you	J. her	P. they
E. your	K. it	Q. them
F. he	L. its	R. their

➾ Practice saying the sentences.

Irregular Verbs with Long Vowel Changes. Modern English has many of the irregular verbs found in Old English. This chapter introduces you to a few more.

Present tense	Past tense	Pronunciation
bring	brought	/ ȯ /
buy	bought	/ ȯ /
drive	drove	/ ō /
find	found	/ aů /
stand	stood*	/ ů /
take	took	/ ů /
sell	sold	/ ō /
tell	told	/ ō /
understand	understood*	/ ů /

* These forms also lose the "n."

➾ Practice saying the words.

Exercise 4.5

Multiple choice. Circle the letter in front of the sentence with the correct form of the past tense verb.

1. A. He finded his keys in the yard.
   B. He found his keys in the yard.
   C. He fint his keys in the yard.
   D. He founded his keys in the yard.

2. A. She bring fried chicken to the picnic.
   B. She bringed fried chicken to the picnic.
   C. She brought fried chicken to the picnic.
   D. She brong fried chicken to the picnic.

3. A. John told Henry a story.
   B. John tell Henry a story.
   C. John telled Henry a story.
   D. John tol Henry a story.

4. A. The manager sell the coat.
   B. The manager selled the coat.
   C. The manager sold the coat.
   D. The manager selld the coat.

5. A. Mike stood by the tree.
   B. Mike standed by the tree.
   C. Mike stooded by the tree.
   D. Mike stands by the tree.

6. A. Todd buy Sally a rose bush.
   B. Todd buyed Sally a rose bush.
   C. Todd boughted Sally a rose bush.
   D. Todd bought Sally a rose bush.

7. A. Sally drived to the park.
   B. Sally drove to the park.
   C. Sally droved to the park.
   D. Sally driven to the park.

8. A. Henry understanded Tim.
   B. Henry understood Tim.
   C. Henry understand Tim.
   D. Henry understooded Tim.

9. A. I took the money.
   B. I taked the money.
   C. I tooked the money.
   D. I take the money.

10. A. He bring a horse to the park.
    B. He bringed a horse to the park.
    C. He brought a horse to the park.
    D. He broughted a horse to the park.

11. A. The horse stood by the duck pond.
    B. The horse stand by the duck pond.
    C. The horse standed by the duck pond.
    D. The horse stands by the duck pond.

12. A. Emma bought shoes at the mall.
    B. Emma buyed shoes at the mall.
    C. Emma buy shoes at the mall.
    D. Emma boughted shoes at the mall.

13. A. Henry driven Emma to the mall.
    B. Henry drove Emma to the mall.
    C. Henry droved Emma to the mall.
    D. Henry drived Emma to the mall.

14. A. She sell cotton candy in the park.
    B. She selled cotton candy in the park.
    C. She seld cotton candy in the park.
    D. She sold cotton candy in the park.

15. A. She found her keys in the road.
    B. She finded her keys in the road.
    C. She find her keys in the road.
    D. She founded her keys in the road.

16. A. He bring peanuts to the store.
    B. He brought peanuts to the store.
    C. He bringed peanuts to the store.
    D. He broughted peanuts to the store.

17. A. I understand English.
    B. I understanded English.
    C. I understooded English.
    D. I understood English.

18. A. They find a dog in Macy's.
    B. They finded a dog in Macy's.
    C. They found a dog in Macy's.
    D. They founded a dog in Macy's.

19. A. The child told a lie.
    B. The child tell a lie.
    C. The child telled a lie.
    D. The child tolded a lie.

20. A. You bringed it on yourself.
    B. You bring it on yourself.
    C. You brought it on yourself.
    D. You broughted it on yourself.

Exercise 4.6

Fill in. Fill in the blanks below with the correct form of the past tense verb.

1. Emma ________ cotton candy for Susan.
   (bring)

2. Susan ________ in line for an hour.
   (stand)

3. Henry ________ a walk in the park.
   (take)

4. John ________ the man a tie.
   (sell)

5. Andrea ________ a coat.
   (buy)

6. I ________ my keys.
   (find)

7. We ________ a truck to Baltimore.
   (drive)

8. They _______ coffee and pastries.
   (sell)

9. I _______ you about him.
(tell)

10. You _____________ me.
(understand)

11. The child ________ still.
(stand)

12. I thought you _________ the hamburgers.
(bring)

13. He _______ biology last semester.
(take)

14. He ________ outside waiting.
(stand)

15. Joong ________ Sarah to the party.
(bring)

➾ Practice saying the sentences.

Speaking. For each of the verb phrases listed below, begin the sentence with an appropriate pronoun and then complete the sentence with the verb phrase. Use every pronoun that agrees with the verb given. Practice saying the list with a partner.

Pronouns as Subjects

I	he	it	we
you	she	they	

1. ate our dinner
   ate their berries
   ate my breakfast

2. bought a hat
   bought a pair of shoes
   bought presents for them

3. didn't know him
   did my homework
   didn't do my homework
   did buy the coat

4. drove you to the park
   drove them to the store
   drove him to the house

5. found my book
   found our house
   found their store

6. lifted his boxes
   lifted my supplies
   lifted her chair

7. remembered his name
   remembered her dog
   remembered my homework

8. stole his shoes
   stole their car
   stole our TV

9. took their classes
   took his potatoes
   took her fries

10. wanted their presents
    wanted her shoes
    wanted to see him

11. went home
    went to the mall
    went to bed

12. wrote an e-mail to him
    wrote a letter to her
    wrote his essay for English

Reading. An e-mail from an English speaker living in America to someone learning English.

Dear Mr. Park,

I am writing to you to tell you about my life. I hope you will write me back and tell me something about yourself.

My name is Emma Hernandez. I was born in the Dominican Republic in 1994, and I am sixteen years old. In 1995, I came to the United States with my father, mother, and brother. My sister Susan was born in 1998 in the United States, which makes her a U.S. citizen. My parents wanted to come to the U.S. because it was hard to get jobs back home. In America, my father manages a luggage store in the local mall, and my mother is a cook at a restaurant in our neighborhood. I am a sophomore at Jefferson High School, and my brother Henry is a freshman at the University of Central California. My sister Susan is in seventh grade at Mariposa Middle School.

I like to go to the mall with my friends. We look at the new clothes. Sometimes we sit in the food court and talk, or see a movie in the movie theater. I love going to the movies. I also like school. My favorite subject is English. I like to write stories and poems. I want to be a writer when I grow up.

I hope you are enjoying your English class, and good luck with your studies. Please write to me soon.

Sincerely,
Ms. Emma Hernandez

Comprehension Activity

1. Why is Ms. Hernandez writing to Mr. Park?
2. Where was she born?
3. How old is she?
4. Where does she live now?
5. Why did she come to America?
6. Where was her sister born?
7. Who is an American citizen?
8. Where does her mother work?
9. Where is her brother a student?
10. What does she love to do?
11. What does she want Mr. Park to do?

Writing Activity. Write an e-mail to Emma telling her about yourself.

E-mails and letters begin with the word "Dear." Next write the name of the person you are writing to. Use her title and family name. "Mr." for a male; "Ms." for a female.

Exceptions. Only use a person's given name and leave out her title in the address ("Dear Emma") if you know that person very well. Use a professional title, for example, "Dr.," if you are addressing a medical doctor or a Ph.D. If you are addressing a public office holder, use the office title: for example, "Sen." for senator.

Your e-mail begins "Dear Ms. Hernandez." Add a comma (,) after her name because you are writing a personal letter. If you were writing for a business or professional purpose, you would use a colon (:) in place of the comma.

The body of the e-mail, or letter, is separated into paragraphs. There is a blank line between pararaphs. The first paragraph explains the reason for the letter. The middle paragraphs give more details; each body paragraph gives a different set of details. Ms. Hernandez talks about where she is from; when she was born; how old she is; her family members; where they live now, and what they do. The last paragraph asks for a response. The letter ends with "Sincerely," on the second to last line, and the letter writer's "signature" on the last line. Signatures include both given name and family name. That is, the first name is the given name, and the last name is the family name for Westerners. For East Asians, the first name is the family name, and the last name is the given name.

When you write your letter, follow Ms. Hernandez's pattern of topics. In addition, follow her visual format. That is, use the margins, locations of things, and white space exactly the same way.

Chapter 5: Talking to a Professor

Grammar

Adjectives and Articles, Comparative and Superlative.

Dialogue

Dialogue for pronunciation and intonation. The teacher reads to the class, emphasizing pronunciation and intonation. The teacher reads Dr. Jones' part while students read Kim's part. Students pair up and practice the dialogue, and then switch parts and practice again. The teacher corrects pronunciation and intonation.

Kim	Hi, Dr. Jones. Is this a good time? I know your office hours are over.
Dr. Jones	It's OK. Come in. What's up?
Kim	I have to write a research paper for English class. It's open topic: I can write on anything I want.
Dr. Jones	OK.
Kim	I'm supposed to interview a professor. Well, I want to interview you, if I can.
Dr. Jones	Sure, OK. How long will this take?
Kim	Oh, I'm not sure. Probably just fifteen minutes.
Dr. Jones	OK. I've got a faculty meeting in half an hour. We could do this now if you're ready.
Kim	Oh, great! Thanks. I want to know what you think about water conservation.
Dr. Jones	Could you tell me what you've been reading, or what interests you about water conservation?
Kim	Well, you know I work for Ms. Weiss here on campus. We take care of the landscaping. She said we have to stop planting rye grass in the winter and just let the lawns die. So, I said I thought it would look ugly.
Dr. Jones	And she told you the campus needs to conserve water.

Kim	Oh, well, yeah. But all these claims about the planet drying up, or whatever, doesn't it seem pretty silly? I mean, there's water everywhere! Most of the faucets on campus drip water. The sprinklers are broken in places, and they spray water into the street. The coffee shops leave water running all day just to rinse their spoons. There must be tons of water everywhere if we can do all that.
Dr. Jones	So, you're saying you believe that there is an abundance of water on the planet because people waste it?
Kim	Uh, yeah.
Dr. Jones	So, people wouldn't waste water unless there were an abundance of it?
Kim	Right.
Dr. Jones	Let's try an analogy. Do you think people would spend money if they didn't have it?
Kim	Smart people wouldn't.
Dr. Jones	Are people always smart about money?
Kim	I think most people are.
Dr. Jones	Most people consider how much money they have before they buy things.
Kim	Well, my parents do. My brother doesn't. He bought a new stereo for his car before he paid his university fees this semester. He had to borrow money from Dad. Last year I bought a cute pair of heels before I bought my ticket to see Pink with my friends. Darryl let me pay him back later, though.
Dr. Jones	So, do people always conserve resources when they are in short supply?
Kim	Smart people do.
Dr. Jones	If people are not always smart about their own money, do you think they are likely to be smarter about a shared resource like water?
Kim	What do you mean?
Dr. Jones	Water comes out of faucets. When we turn on the faucet, we don't know how much water there is, nor do we know how much water other people are using.
Kim	Oh, so it's like if you don't know how much money you have in the bank. You just keep spending it until you realize that it's gone.
Dr. Jones	I think so.
Kim	OK, but somebody must know how much water is left, or no one would say we need to conserve it.

Dr. Jones It sounds like you're ready to go to the library and do some research. You can come back Thursday during my office hours if you have more questions then.

Kim Thanks, Dr. Jones. I'll get to the library, and I'll see you on Thursday.

Dr. Jones Good luck. See you soon.

Vocabulary

✓ Adjectives

big
clean
cute
good
new
short
silly
smart
ugly
little

long
more
most
much
open
past
ready
shared
smarter
sure
too much
true
broken
fifteen
less

Adjectives describe nouns. They usually come before the nouns they describe: for example, "*Smart* people do." Yet, sometimes adjectives come after the subject and the linking verb: "They are *smart*."

Practice saying these two sentences using each of the adjectives in the first column: "________ people do," and "They are ___________."

✓ Nouns

abundance
analogy
bank

claim
coffee shop
English class

faculty
faucet
half an hour
hour
interview
library
meeting
minute
office
parent
people
place
planet
professor
research paper
resource
rye grass
semester
spoon
sprinkler
stereo
street
ticket
ton
topic
university fee
winter

✓ Indefinite Pronouns

all
anything
everywhere
no one
somebody
whatever

Personal pronouns *I*, *we*, and *they*, for example, stand in for persons we know. Indefinite pronouns stand in for people and things that we don't know about, nonspecific people or things.

✓ Verbs

believe
borrow
can
conserve
consider
drip
leave
mean
must
pay
realize
rinse
say
see
seem
spend
spray
suggest
turn
waste

Exercise 5.1

Multiple Choice. Circle the letter in front of the sentence with the correct word order.

1. A. The smart woman took the bus.
   B. The woman smart took the bus.
   C. The woman smart the bus took.
   D. The smart woman the bus took.

2. A. She the cute pants bought.
   B. She bought the pants cute.
   C. She bought the cute pants.
   D. She the pants cute bought.

3. A. I don't broken want the chair.
   B. I the broken chair don't want.
   C. I the chair broken don't want.
   D. I don't want the broken chair.

4. A. Water clean is everywhere.
   B. Clean water is everywhere.
   C. Clean water everywhere is.
   D. Water clean everywhere is.

5. A. They drove a clean car.
   B. They a clean car drove.
   C. They drove a car clean.
   D. They a car clean drove.

6. A. We the shared equipment borrowed.
   B. We borrowed the shared equipment.
   C. We borrowed the equipment shared.
   D. We the equipment shared borrowed.

7. A. Jill is Euro American.
   B. Jill Euro American is.
   C. Euro American is Jill.
   D. Euro American Jill is.

8. A. Panda bears in big zoos live.
   B. Panda bears live in zoos big.
   C. Panda bears live in big zoos.
   D. Bears panda live in big zoos.

9. A. They little the children are.
   B. They are the children little.
   C. They are the little children.
   D. Are they the little children.

10. A. She is ready for class.
    B. She ready for class is.
    C. She ready is for class.
    D. For class she is ready.

11. A. She saw the tree ugly.
    B. She the ugly tree saw.
    C. She the tree ugly saw.
    D. She saw the ugly tree.

12. A. People fifteen went to work.
    B. Fifteen people went to work.
    C. Fifteen people to work went.
    D. People fifteen to work went.

13. A. The city dry was.
    B. The city was dry.
    C. The dry was city.
    D. Dry was the city.

14. A. The rice hot is.
    B. The rice is hot.
    C. Hot the rice is.
    D. Hot the is rice.

15. A. The story is true.
    B. The story true is.
    C. True is the story.
    D. True the story is.

16. A. I wrote a paper long.
    B. I a long paper wrote.
    C. I a paper long wrote.
    D. I wrote a long paper.

17. A. She told a story silly.
    B. She a silly story told.
    C. Told she a silly story.
    D. She told a silly story.

18. A. We in a shared house live.
    B. We in a house shared live.
    C. We live in a shared house.
    D. We live in a house shared.

19. A. He wanted a office new.
    B. He wanted a new office.
    C. He a new office wanted.
    D. He a office new wanted.

20. A. Todd has a life better.
    B. Todd a better life has.
    C. Todd has a better life.
    D. Todd a life better has.

21. A. I am about it sure.
    B. I am sure about it.
    C. I sure about it am.
    D. I sure am about it.

22. A. He walked a path narrow.
    B. He walked a narrow path.
    C. He a narrow path walked.
    D. He a path narrow walked.

23. A. Sally Jewish American is.
    B. Is Sally Jewish American.
    C. Sally is Jewish American.
    D. Jewish American is Sally.

24. A. Mike tall man a is.
    B. Mike is a tall man.
    C. Mike a tall man is.
    D. Mike is a man tall.

25. A. Mike is African American.
    B. Mike African American is.
    C. Is Mike African American.
    D. African American is Mike.

Comparative and Superlative Adjectives. Adjectives have three forms: the base form, the comparative, and the superlative. The base gives a detail about the noun it describes. The comparative indicates that one noun has more of that quality than another noun. The superlative indicates it has the most of that quality among three or more nouns. The comparative is used when comparing two things. Most adjectives become comparative by adding "er" to the ending. Most adjectives become superlative by adding "est."

Base	Comparative	Superlative
new	newer	newest
old	older	oldest
fresh	fresher	freshest
stale	staler	stalest
smart	smarter	smartest
dumb	dumber	dumbest
big	bigger	biggest
small	smaller	smallest
broad	broader	broadest
narrow	narrower	narrowest
tall	taller	tallest
long	longer	longest
short	shorter	shortest
close	closer	closest
far	farther	farthest
clean	cleaner	cleanest
messy	messier	messiest
cute	cuter	cutest
ugly	uglier	ugliest
hard	harder	hardest
soft	softer	softest
dark	darker	darkest
light	lighter	lightest
hot	hotter	hottest
cold	colder	coldest
spicy	spicier	spiciest
bland	blander	blandest
nice	nicer	nicest
mean	meaner	meanest

The list of adjectives above is arranged in the order of paired opposites. The word *than* is often used with the comparative form, and *of* with the superlative. For example:

- John is nice, but Mike is nicer *than* John, and Sang-hee is the nicest *of* the three.
- Sang-hee is mean, but Mike is meaner *than* Sang-hee, and John is the meanest *of* the three.
- Barbecued chicken is spicy, but chili is spicier *than* barbecue, and ramyeon is the spiciest *of* the three.
- Pizza is bland, but hamburgers are blander *than* pizza, and sesame soup is the blandest *of* the three.

Now you will write some sentences like these.

Partner Writing and Speaking Excercise. Partners choose one of the categories below and brainstorm a list of ten items that you can compare. Next, write five sentences that follow the models above using the comparative and superlative forms of the adjectives in the list. Practice saying your sentences together and prepare to say them to the class.

Categories:

Transportation:	Food:	Clothing:
cars	dishes	shoes
buses	restaurants	suits
trains	national cuisines	dress clothing
planes	best / worst meals	casual clothing

Academics:	Entertainment:	Music:
college majors	books	genres
colleges classes	movies	artists
universities	TV shows	instruments
education	concerts	performances

Long comparative and superlative adjectives do not have endings. Instead, "more" comes in front of the adjective to form the comparative, and "most" in front of the adjective to form the superlative.

Base	Comparative	Superlative
beautiful	more beautiful	most beautiful
prepared	more prepared	most prepared
open	more open	most open
savory	more savory	most savory

In general, "more" and "most" are used in front of adjectives with three or more syllables, but several two-syllable adjectives also require more and most. Consult a dictionary to be sure: *-er* and *–est* are in dictionary entries for those that take them. Practice saying the phrases.

Less and Least. Adjectives may also be used to indicate that a person or item has less of a quality than another. Long adjectives have "less" and "least" in front of them.

Base	Comparative	Superlative
beautiful	less beautiful	least beautiful
prepared	less prepared	least prepared
open	less open	least open
savory	less savory	least savory

Practice saying the phrases.

Short adjectives have "not as ________ as" for the comparative.

- *Dave is not as big as Mike.*
- *Your ramyeon is not as spicy as my ramyeon.*
- *John is not as young as Henry.*

The superlative indicating a lesser quality is rarely used for short adjectives. Instead, the opposite adjective is used in the positive. So, if you want to say that Joong is the least tall of the men, instead say, "Joong is the shortest of the men." Also, not "Jill's eggs are the least spicy," but instead "Jill's eggs are the blandest" is correct.

Irregular Adjectives. A few adjectives are irregular and very commonly used.

Base	Comparative	Superlative
good	better	best
bad	worse	worst
many	more	most
much	more	most
some	more	most
little	less, littler	least, littlest

Practice saying the words. "Many" and "much" indicate a large amount. "Many" describes nouns that can be counted, like people, dogs, hats, houses, and cars. "Much" is used with nouns that are not countable in English, like water, rice, furniture, and chalk. Some nouns that are noncountable in English may be countable in other languages. So, you will have to memorize the non-countable nouns to choose the right adjective.

Less and littler are also used differently. This is because "little" can mean two different things.

- The *little* child likes dessert.
- We have *little* money.

The child is small. If we were to compare children, we could say, "Peter is little, but Mary is littler." On the other hand, "little money" is not a size but an amount. "We have little money, but they have less money than we do." Practice saying the sentences.

Exercise 5.2

Multiple Choice. Circle the letter in front of the sentence with the correct adjective and word order.

1. A. Andrea is taller than Jill.
   B. Andrea is tall than Jill.
   C. Andrea is tallest than Jill.
   D. Andrea taller than Jill is.

2. A. Tim is close than Kim.
   B. Tim is closest than Kim.
   C. Tim is closer than Kim.
   D. Tim closer than Kim is.

3. A. The maples are the harder of all these trees.
   B. The maples are the hardest of all these trees.
   C. The maples are the hard of all these trees.
   D. The maples the harder of all these trees are.

4. A. Mike's 2010 Honda is the new of all the cars.
   B. Mike's 2010 Honda is the newest of all the cars.
   C. Mike's 2010 Honda is the newer of all the cars.
   D. Mike's 2010 Honda the newest of all the cars is.

5. A. Your face is narrowest than my face.
   B. Your face is narrow than my face.
   C. Your face is narrower than my face.
   D. Your face narrower than my face is.

6. A. His legs longer are than her legs.
   B. His legs are longer than her legs.
   C. His legs are more long than her legs.
   D. His legs are longest than her legs.

7. A. Joong is the nice person of his family.
   B. Joong is the nicer person of his family.
   C. Joong is the nicest person of his family.
   D. Joong the nicest person is of his family.

8. A. That is the cutest dog in the park.
   B. That is the cuter dog in the park.
   C. That is the cute dog in the park.
   D. That the cute dog in the park is.

9. A. Todd has the pretty yard of all the neighbors.
   B. Todd has the most pretty yard of all the neighbors.
   C. Todd has the prettier yard of all the neighbors.
   D. Todd has the prettiest yard of all the neighbors.

10. A. Huntington Lake is the most beautiful.
    B. Huntington Lake is the beautifullest.
    C. Huntington Lake the most beautiful is.
    D. Huntington Lake the beautifullest is.

11. A. Tim was prepareder that day than I.
    B. Tim was more prepared that day than I.
    C. He prepareder that day than I was.
    D. He was most prepared that day than I.

12. A. Sesame soup is the most bland soup.
    B. Sesame soup is the blandest soup.
    C. Sesame soup most bland the is.
    D. Sesame soup the most bland is.

13. A. The biggest tree in the park was on the corner.
    B. The most big tree in the park was on the corner.
    C. The most big tree in the park on the corner was.
    D. The biggest tree in the park on the corner was.

14. A. The meanest of the two ducks the dog bit.
    B. The most mean of the two ducks bit the dog.
    C. The more mean of the two ducks bit the dog.
    D. The meaner of the two ducks bit the dog.

15. A. *The Lord of the Ring*s the longest movie was I saw.
    B. *The Lord of the Rings* was the most long movie I saw.
    C. *The Lord of the Rings* was the longest movie I saw.
    D. *The Lord of the Rings* the longest movie I saw was.

16. A. Sarah has the messiest desk on campus.
    B. Sarah the messiest desk has on campus.
    C. Sarah has the most messy desk on campus.
    D. Sarah the most messy desk on campus has.

17. A. Stella was the beautifullest woman at the party.
    B. Stella the most beautiful woman was at the party.
    C. Stella the beautifullest woman was at the party.
    D. Stella was the most beautiful woman at the party.

18. A. Peet's is the most clean coffee shop in Sacramento.
    B. Peet's the cleanest coffee shop is in Sacramento.
    C. Peet's is the cleanest coffee shop in Sacramento.
    D. Peet's the most clean coffee shop is in Sacramento.

19. A. Henry's shoes darker are than Emma's.
    B. Henry's shoes are more dark than Emma's.
    C. Henry's shoes are darker than Emma's.
    D. Henry's shoes darker than Emma's are.

20. A. He made a bad decision.
    B. He made a worse decision.
    C. He made a worst decision.
    D. He a bad decision made.

21. A. The bathroom is the coldest room in the house.
    B. The bathroom is the colder room in the house.
    C. The bathroom the room coldest in the house is.
    D. The bathroom coldest the room is in the house.

22. A. Susan's bed is softer than Emma's bed.
    B. Susan's bed is soft than Emma's bed.
    C. Susan's bed is softest than Emma's bed.
    D. Susan's bed is more soft than Emma's bed.

23. A. Todd more for his trees paid than for his bushes.
    B. Todd paid much for his trees than for his bushes.
    C. Todd paid most for his trees than for his bushes.
    D. Todd paid more for his trees than for his bushes.

24. A. He owes you more money than I do.
    B. He owes you most money than I do.
    C. He owes you many money than I do.
    D. He owes you much money than I do.

25. A. Children like dessert good than dinner.
    B. Children like dessert best than dinner.
    C. Children like dessert much than dinner.
    D. Children like dessert better than dinner.

Irregular verbs that don't change spelling. Most of these are also pronounced the same in both tenses, but note "read."

Present tense	Past tense, all subjects	Pronunciation
bet	bet	/ bet /
read / rēd / *	read	/ red /
cut	cut	/ cət /
hurt	hurt	/ hərt /
hit	hit	/ hit /
quit	quit	/ kwit /
cost	cost	/ cȯst /
put	put	/ pu̇t /

Present tense "read" is pronounced / ē /, but past tense "read" is pronounced / e / . Practice saying the words. In the past tense, even the 3rd person singular takes the base form.

Present tense	Past tense
He cuts the steak.	*He cut the steak.*
It hurts to walk.	*It hurt to walk.*

Practice saying the sentences.

Exercise 5.3

Rewrite the following sentences in the past tense.

1. She hits the ball harder than he does.

___

2. Mike puts more chicken on the grill.

___

3. The mean man hits the black table the hardest.

___

4. Darryl reads the longest book on the syllabus.

___

5. Mrs. Hernandez bets the most money on the horse.

___

6. You set the spicy chicken on the table.

___

7. John sets the sweetest oranges on the desk.

___

8. They bet little money you would win.

___

9. Dave quits for the day.

___

10. Kim's textbooks cost three hundred dollars.

___

11. The sandwich costs little money.

___

12. We put our closest friends on the list.

___

13. Todd puts his boat on the farther shore.

____

14. Emma reads a happy story to the sad child.

____

15. Sang-hee quits smoking cold turkey.

____

16. Emma reads novels in the bedroom.

____

17. Mike's car costs a lot of money.

____

18. Sally sets the tools on the bench.

____

19. You cut the chicken.

____

➾ Practice saying the sentences.

Articles. There are only three articles in the English language, but they are used the most frequently of all words.

Articles	Pronunciation
a	/ ə / ā /
an	/ ăn /
the	/ ðə / ðē / (voiced th)

➾ Practice saying the articles. "An" is always pronounced the same. "A" is usually pronounced /ə/, but is pronounced /ā/ sometimes for emphasis. "The" is usually pronounced /ðə/, but is pronounced /ðē/ sometimes for emphasis or in front of a word that begins with a vowel.

Articles go in front of nouns.

- *The* is a definite article. It is used to specify which thing or things among different things. For example, "I want the sandwich" means I am choosing the sandwich, not the hamburger, or the bowl of soup.
- *A* is an indefinite article that can only be used in front of singular nouns. It is used when any one of something will do. For example, "I want a sandwich." I am not making a choice among different things.
- *An* is an indefinite article that can only be used in front of singular nouns, the same as *a*. *A* is used when the next word begins with a consonant sound; *an* is used when the next word begins with a vowel sound. For example, *a* is used before sandwich, but *an* is used before egg: "I want a sandwich"; "I want an egg."

Consonant Sound		Vowel Sound	
a banana	/ b /	*an* apple	/ ă /
a spice	/ sp /	*an* herb*	/ ĕr /
a history class*	/ hĭ /	*an* English class	/ ĕng /
a universe*	/ yū /	*an* umbrella*	/ ŭm /

➾ Practice saying the phrases.

* The choice of *a* or *an* depends on the sound at the beginning of the next word. It does not depend on the letter the next word begins with.

Exercise 5.4

Multiple Choice. Circle the letter in front of the sentence with the correct use, or correct lack, of the article.

1. A. Let's go to movie theater across the street.
   B. Let's go to the movie theater across the street.
   C. Let's go to a movie theater across the street.
   D. Let's go to a movie theaters across the street.

2. A. We didn't like the movie we saw last night.
   B. We didn't like a movie we saw last night.
   C. We didn't like an movie we saw last night.
   D. We didn't like movie we saw last night.

3. A. She is a woman I was telling you about.
   B. She is an woman I was telling you about.
   C. She is the woman I was telling you about.
   D. She is woman I was telling you about.

4. A. Kim wrote research paper on environment.
   B. Kim wrote an research paper on a environment.
   C. Kim wrote a research paper on an environment.
   D. Kim wrote the research paper on the environment.

5. A. Dr. Jones bought a concert ticket.
   B. Dr. Jones bought concert ticket.
   C. Dr. Jones bought the concert ticket.
   D. Dr. Jones bought an concert ticket.

6. A. Henry is going to bank to withdraw his money.
   B. Henry is going to an bank to withdraw his money.
   C. Henry is going to the bank to withdraw his money.
   D. Henry is going to a bank to withdraw his money.

7. A. I have always loved roses.
   B. I have always loved an roses.
   C. I have always loved the roses.
   D. I have always loved a roses.

8. A. Most cars weigh more than the ton.
   B. Most cars weigh more than a ton.
   C. Most cars weigh more than ton.
   D. Most cars weigh more than an ton.

9. A. She can't pay university fee.
   B. She can't pay a university fee.
   C. She can't pay an university fee.
   D. She can't pay the university fee.

10. A. Semester is over.
    B. The semester is over.
    C. A semester is over.
    D. An semester is over.

11. A. A board meeting is today at 2:30 p.m..
    B. Board meeting is today at 2:30 p.m..
    C. The board meeting is today at 2:30 p.m..
    D. An board meeting is today at 2:30 p.m..

12. A. I can meet you in a hour.
    B. I can meet you in an hour.
    C. I can meet you in the hour.
    D. I can meet you in hour.

13. A. I always keep my keys in the same place.
    B. I always keep my keys in a same place.
    C. I always keep my keys in an same place.
    D. I always keep my keys in same place.

14. A. Government would not let people speak freely.
    B. The government would not let the people speak freely.
    C. A government would not let a people speak freely.
    D. An government would not let an people speak freely.

15. A. I dress warm in the winter.
    B. I dress warm in winter.
    C. I dress warm in a winter.
    D. I dress warm in an winter.

16. A. This is best ice cream I've ever had.
    B. This is a best ice cream I've ever had.
    C. This is an best ice cream I've ever had.
    D. This is the best ice cream I've ever had.

17. A. I can have an orange from her tree.
    B. I can have a orange from her tree.
    C. I can have the orange from her tree.
    D. I can have orange from her tree.

18. A. I need a spoon to eat this.
    B. I need an spoon to eat this.
    C. I need spoon to eat this.
    D. I need the spoon to eat this.

19. A. My uncle lives across a street.
    B. My uncle lives across an street.
    C. My uncle lives across street.
    D. My uncle lives across the street.

20. A. I have never liked pizza.
    B. I have never liked the pizza.
    C. I have never liked a pizza.
    D. I have never liked an pizza.

21. A. Dr. Jones used analogy to explain water conservation.
    B. Dr. Jones used the analogy to explain water conservation.
    C. Dr. Jones used a analogy to explain water conservation.
    D. Dr. Jones used an analogy to explain water conservation.

22. A. My favorite movie is *Alien*.
    B. My favorite movie is the *Alien*.
    C. My favorite movie is a *Alien*.
    D. My favorite movie is an *Alien*.

23. A. I thought you had job interview today.
    B. I thought you had the job interview today.
    C. I thought you had a job interview today.
    D. I thought you had an job interview today.

24. A. This is one I want.
    B. This is the one I want.
    C. This is a one I want.
    D. This is an one I want.

25. A. Let me see picture.
    B. Let me see the picture.
    C. Let me see a picture.
    D. Let me see an picture.

Exercise 5.5

Fill in. Write the best article (*the, a, or an*) for the context in the blanks.

1. He went to ______ university closest to his house.
2. She wanted ______ apple.
3. ______ man was smart.
4. He saw ______ bird on the beach.
5. He cut ______ biggest steak.
6. They bet on ______ best team.
7. He put on ______ shirt.
8. She broke ______ blue umbrella yesterday.
9. She read ______ best book on the table.
10. He hit ______ oldest baseball out of the park.
11. ______ house cost too much money.
12. He put his money on ______ dining room table.
13. I bet he didn't know ______ woman.
14. He hurt his ankle in ______ soccer game last season.
15. He quit ______ part-time job once a long time ago.

➾ Practice saying the sentences.

Reading. This e-mail was written by a college student to his instructor.

Dear Dr. Jones:

I am a student in your 10 o'clock Monday-Wednesday-Friday biology class. My name is Tim Tapscott. I am writing to tell you about our group project and to ask for your advice and approval.

My group is thinking about building a small koi pond to go inside the arboretum on campus. The pond can give the biology department another resource for study. Students can study the water, the aquatic plants, and the koi. In addition, our campus landscaper Ms. Weiss said it's no problem getting supplies for it in town. She said we won't waste any water, and the aquatic plants would keep it clean. We also think it can make the campus more beautiful.

Can our group meet with you during your office hours Thursday? Ms. Weiss warned us that there are still many details to work out. Also, you can call her to find out about her information. Her cell phone number is 970-6958.

Thanks so much. Your classes have been very inspiring to me. I am very excited about this project; we all are.

Sincerely,
Tim Tapscott

Comprehension activity.

1. Why is Tim Tapscott writing to Dr. Jones?
2. What four things does Tim tell Dr. Jones about himself in the first two sentences?
3. What does his group want to do?
4. Where do they want to do it?
5. What reasons does he give Dr. Jones to get her to approve of the project?
6. Why does he say that he talked to Ms. Weiss?
7. What does he ask for in the third paragraph?
8. Why does he give a cell phone number to Dr. Jones?
9. What is his attitude in the last paragraph?

Writing Activity: Write an e-mail to a professor.

In your e-mail, ask about one or two of the topics below:

- a class concept or skill you do not understand fully.
- your progress in the class.
- permission to write your paper, or do your presentation or project, on a specific topic.
- the topic you have chosen for a paper, presentation, or group project.
- if you can make up an assignment that you missed.
- follow-up questions about a class you missed.

Begin with a salutation, Dear Professor, followed by his or her family name. End with a closing, Sincerely, followed by your name (given name and family name in whichever order is appropriate to the situation). Write your letter in paragraphs, each with its own topic and purpose. For more details, see the writing assignment in chapter 4.

Chapter 6: Talking About Television

Grammar

Word Order for Noun Phrases, Proper Nouns, Intensive, Reflexive, and Demonstrative Pronouns.

Dialogue

Dialogue for pronunciation and intonation. The teacher reads to the class, emphasizing pronunciation and intonation. The teacher reads Andrea's part while students read Jill's part. Students pair up and practice the dialogue, and then switch parts and practice again. The teacher corrects pronunciation and intonation.

Andrea	Thank you for choosing Starbucks. Can I get you a mocha frappuccino?
Jill	Hi, Andrea. How's it going?
Andrea	It's a slow day. Did you see *Castle* last week?
Jill	You mean that new TV show with Nathan Fillion? Yeah, I love him. Alyssa Milano was on. She portrayed his ex-girlfriend.
Andrea	Detective Beckett wanted her to be guilty of the murder. She's so jealous of the competition.
Jill	Maybe, I don't know.
Andrea	She told Castle not to spend time with her.
Jill	She was a suspect. The police are supposed to be unbiased.
Andrea	(To a drive-through customer) Thank you for choosing Starbucks. Can I get you a mocha frappuccino? (Pause) Can I get you a pastry with that?
Jill	Did she say grande?
Andrea	Um, grande vanilla latte and a maple scone. I got the scone.
Jill	OK. Did you see the *Golden Globe Awards* last night?
Andrea	I heard *Avatar* won for best film.
Jill	It did. Did you see it? Did you like it?
Andrea	Oh, yeah. I don't go to the movies much now that it costs so much, but my cousin told me it was really worth the money. It was a great film. I'd go see it again.
Jill	I guess I'll see it on DVD.

Andrea It's a three-D movie. It won't be the same. When you see those characters fly off the cliff and swoop around, it feels like they're going to run right into you.

Jill Wow, I didn't know that. Maybe I'll ask Tim if he wants to go. I don't like going by myself.

Andrea You mean Tim hasn't seen it yet? I thought he took Kim.

Jill No, he's working on a project for biology. It's taking all his time.

Andrea Oh. He's really serious about that class. Is he doing all the work himself?

Jill No, he's leading a group from his class.

Andrea Do you want me to clean the pastry case?

Jill Go ahead. I'll watch the drive-through.

Andrea Thanks. Wow, look at those clouds outside!

Jill Hm? Oh!

Andrea It's going to rain.

Jill Skip the pastry case for now. Take those umbrellas off the patio.

Andrea OK. I can do it myself.

Jill (To a drive-through customer) Thank you for choosing Starbucks. Can I get you a mocha frappuccino? (Pause) Can I get you a pastry with that?

Andrea I got the cappuccino.

Jill Thanks. Extra dry.

Andrea Yes. Have you seen *Glee*?

Jill The show about the high school glee club? No. I was in the chorus in high school, and I'm still trying to forget the experience.

Andrea You like music. You might like this show. It's got two or three production numbers per show, and each one is about the plot, or how one of the characters feels. It's like seeing a musical every week.

Jill I heard the characters in the glee club were really nerdy and were teased all the time.

Andrea That happened in the first episode, but the glee club got more confidence, and more kids joined the club. They started to take good care of each other. It's kind of sweet. I was hoping the show would win a *Golden Globe*.

Jill Oh, it did. I saw that last night. I was kind of surprised. Musicals are really unpopular.

Andrea Awesome! (Pause.) It's raining outside.

Jill Did you sing in high school?

Andrea Yes. I sing now.

Jill Really? Are you taking music classes in college?

Andrea	I sing tribal songs with my family.
Jill	Oh, cool. That must be really exciting.
Andrea	It's really hard, but it's nice to sing together. Anyone in the tribe can join us, but it's usually certain families that play music. My family does.
Jill	I've never heard Native American music.
Andrea	No one has. OK, not really. You can hear Native American music on KPFA. There's a native program on Tuesdays at 3 o'clock.
Jill	KPFA?
Andrea	It's a public radio station. Eighty-eight-point-one, FM radio.
Jill	Never heard of it. Wow. Thanks. I'll have to listen to it some time.
Andrea	(To a customer in the store) Thank you for choosing Starbucks. Can I get you a mocha frappuccino?

Vocabulary

✓ Nouns

ex-girlfriend
cappuccino
characters
chorus
cliff
cloud
competition
confidence
customer
day
drive-through
DVD
episode
experience
film
glee club
high school
last night
latte
mocha
movies
music
musical
night
pastry
pastry case
patio
plot
police
production number
radio station
scone
show
suspect
umbrella
vanilla
week
work

✐ Adjectives

certain
dry
great
guilty
jealous
maple
Native American
nerdy
public
serious
slow
surprised
sweet
tribal
unbiased
unpopular

✐ Verbs

choose
feel
fly
forget
go (ahead)*
guess
heard
hope
join
lead
listen
look
love
mean
play (music)
portray
rain
sing
skip
supposed (to be)
swoop
take (care of)*
tease
thank
try
watch

*See Chapter 10 on phrasal verbs.

A proper noun is always capitalized because it is a name. A common noun like "coffee shop" is not capitalized, but "Starbucks" is capitalized. "The professor" is not capitalized, but "Professor Jones" is.

✐ Proper Nouns

Alyssa Milano
Andrea
Avatar
Castle
*Castle**
Detective Beckett
Glee
Golden Globe Awards
Nathan Fillion
Starbucks

*The names of television shows and books are in italics. This helps readers see the difference between the show *Castle* and the character Castle.

A pronoun is a word that takes the place of a noun. For example, personal pronouns *he*, *she*, and *they* take the place of a particular person or persons. (See chapter 4 for more details.) Demonstrative pronouns identify or emphasize certain persons, places, or things.

✓ **Demonstrative Pronouns**

Singular	Plural
this	these (first, more immediate, or close things)
that	those (second, later, or things farther away)

This man is taller than *that* one.
This is the man you are looking for.
That is not his car.

➾ Practice saying the sentences.

✓ **Noun phrases**. A noun phrase includes a noun and all the words describing it. The article, or demonstrative or possessive pronoun, comes first. The adjective comes right before the noun. The noun comes last.

- I like *the musical show*.
- He watches *that comedy show*.
- She drives *her blue Mercedes Benz convertible*.
- *The tallest building* in New York is across the street.
- He thinks *the shortest books* are the best ones.

The stress within a noun phrase falls on the noun at the end. Practice saying the sentences.

Exercise 6.1

Multiple choice. Circle the letter in front of the sentence with the correct word order.

1. A. She saw *Twilight* with her boyfriend.
   B. She saw *Twilight* with boyfriend her.
   C. She her *Twilight* with boyfriend saw.
   D. She saw *Twilight* boyfriend her with.

2. A. He went to Starbucks for mocha a.
   B. He went to Starbucks a for mocha.
   C. He went to Starbucks for a mocha.
   D. He to Starbucks for a mocha went.

3. A. Mike walked dog his to the park.
   B. Mike walked his dog to park the.
   C. Mike walked dog his to park the.
   D. Mike walked his dog to the park.

4. A. She sang in good chorus the.
   B. She sang in the chorus good.
   C. She sang in the good chorus.
   D. She sang in good the chorus.

5. A. Man the Native American came to store the.
   B. The Native American man came to the store.
   C. The man Native American came to the store.
   D. The Native man American came to the store.

6. A. The professors have a meeting in half an hour.
   B. Professors the have meeting a in half an hour.
   C. Professors the a meeting in half an hour have.
   D. The professors a meeting in half an hour have.

7. A. I never saw the show serious with Nathan Fillion.
   B. I never saw serious show the with Nathan Fillion.
   C. I never saw serious the show with Nathan Fillion.
   D. I never saw the serious show with Nathan Fillion.

8. A. My sister watches TV with her friends.
   B. Sister my watches TV with friends her.
   C. My sister TV her friends watches with.
   D. My sister watches TV with friends her.

9. A. Mike listens to music slow.
   B. Mike listens to slow music.
   C. Mike to slow music listens.
   D. Mike to music slow listens.

10. A. The woman smart saves her money.
    B. The woman smart money her saves.
    C. Woman the smart saves money her.
    D. The smart woman saves her money.

11. A. Joong took his cousins to the movies.
    B. Joong took cousins his to movies the.
    C. Joong his cousins to the movies took.
    D. Joong cousins his to movies the took.

12. A. She thanked Jill for scone the.
    B. She thanked Jill for the scone.
    C. She Jill for the scone thanked.
    D. She Jill for scone the thanked.

13. A. Bird gray the swooped in front of car the.
    B. The gray bird swooped in front of the car.
    C. The bird gray swooped in front of the car.
    D. Bird the gray swooped in front of car the.

14. A. Andrea felt the rain soft on her face.
    B. Andrea felt the soft rain on her face.
    C. Andrea felt the soft rain on face her.
    D. Andrea the rain soft on her face felt.

15. A. Henry loved new experience the.
    B. Henry loved the experience new.
    C. Henry loved experience the new.
    D. Henry loved the new experience.

16. A. Seemed to be everywhere clouds gray.
    B. Clouds gray seemed to be everywhere.
    C. Gray clouds to be everywhere seemed.
    D. Gray clouds seemed to be everywhere.

17. A. Dr. An told students her best to write an e-mail.
    B. Dr. An told best her students to write an e-mail.
    C. Dr. An told her best students to write an e-mail.
    D. Dr. An her best students to write an e-mail told.

18. A. We watched *Glee* week this.
    B. We *Glee* this week watched.
    C. We this week watched *Glee*.
    D. We watched *Glee* this week.

19. A. I heard Native American those songs.
    B. I heard Native American songs those.
    C. I songs those Native American heard.
    D. I heard those Native American songs.

20. A. The police thought man the young was guilty.
    B. The police thought the man young was guilty.
    C. The police thought young man the was guilty.
    D. The police thought the young man was guilty.

21. A. Dog the smart found ball the.
    B. The dog smart found the ball.
    C. Smart dog the found ball the.
    D. The smart dog found the ball.

22. A. These gray clouds mean a rainy day.
    B. Clouds these gray mean day a rainy.
    C. Gray clouds these mean rainy day a.
    D. These gray clouds a rainy day mean.

23. A. These scones maple are popular.
    B. These popular are maple scones.
    C. These maple scones are popular.
    D. Scones these maple are popular.

24. A. Week this slow ends tomorrow.
    B. Week slow this ends tomorrow.
    C. This week slow ends tomorrow.
    D. This slow week ends tomorrow.

25. A. He looks at his tired arms.
    B. He looks at his arms tired.
    C. He looks at arms his tired.
    D. He looks at tired arms his.

Exercise 6.2

Sentence Building. Write the sentences in the correct order, including subject-verb-object and noun phrase order (article / demonstrative or possessive pronoun / adjective / noun). Make sure the first letter of each sentence is capitalized, and the sentence ends in a period.

1. Dr. Jones / students / the / biology / homework / gave

   ____

2. Andrea / cats / black / likes

   ____

3. Jill / movie / scary / the / saw

   ____

4. Todd / yard / big / the / watered

   ____

5. tree / tallest / the / here / stood

   ____

6. Tim and Kim / hardest / the / studied

   ____

7. John and Henry / store / big / the / went to

   ____

8. they / cupcakes / sweet / the / ate

   ____

9. dog / yellow / the / balls / the / found

   ____

10. we / car / fast / a / drove

    ____

11. Emma and Susan / potato salad / salty / the / made

    ____

12. John and Sang-hee / cake / chocolate / the / baked

____

13. Andrea and Jill / cappuccinos / hot / the / drank

____

14. onions / these / sweetest / the / are

____

15. dog / that / balls / hates

____

Stress within a noun phrase falls on the noun at the end. Practice saying the sentences.

✐ Intensive and Reflexive Pronouns

1st sing.	myself	*1st pl.*	ourselves
2nd sing.	yourself	*2nd pl.*	yourselves
3rd sing.	himself / herself / itself	*3rd pl.*	themselves

Intensive Pronouns can emphasize the role of the agent. They come right after the subject to emphasize who is doing the action:

- Tim *himself* did the biology project.
- Andrea *herself* got the umbrellas.
- I *myself* wrote the book.

Intensive pronouns come after the object of the verb to emphasize that the agent completes the action without help:

- Tim did the biology project *himself.*
- Andrea got the umbrellas *herself.*
- I wrote the book *myself.*

There is stress on intensive pronouns. Practice saying the sentences with the stress on the intensive pronouns.

Reflexive Pronouns indicate that the agent of the action is also the receiver. They come after the verb:

- He hurt *himself* playing soccer.
- She cut *herself* chopping potatoes.
- They blamed *themselves* for the boy's death.
- I told *myself* I can do it.
- We found *ourselves* unpopular.
- You punish *yourself* too much.

There is stress on the verb before the reflexive pronoun. Practice saying the sentences with stress on the verb.

F to V. Most modern English words ending in "f" or "fe" originate in Old English and change to "v" / "ve" when an ending is added, such as the "s" ending for the plural form.

Singular	Plural
yourself	yourselves
one knife	forty knives
one leaf	fifty leaves
one life	sixty lives
one thief	seventy thieves
one wolf	eighty wolves
one loaf	ninety loaves (of bread)

Practice saying the words.

Exercise 6.3

Multiple choice. Circle the letter in front of the sentence with the correct pronouns and word order.

1. A. She saw herself in the mirror.
   B. She saw herselves in the mirror.
   C. She saw her in the mirror.
   D. She saw she in the mirror.

2. A. Sang-hee did the work herself.
   B. Sang-hee did the work her.
   C. Sang-hee did the work she.
   D. Sang-hee did the work themselves.

3. A. He watched herself on TV.
   B. He watched herselves on TV.
   C. He watched she on TV.
   D. He watched her on TV.

4. A. That was they dog.
   B. That was their dog.
   C. That was them dog.
   D. That was themselves dog.

5. A. Her made a cup of coffee.
   B. Herself made a cup of coffee.
   C. She made a cup of coffee.
   D. Made her a cup of coffee.

6. A. Those two knives are his.
   B. Those knives two are his.
   C. Those two knives are himself.
   D. Those two knives himself are.

7. A. They told the story themselfs.
   B. Them told the story themselfs.
   C. They the story themself told.
   D. They told the story themselves.

8. A. She saved their lives.
   B. She saved their lifes.
   C. She saved themselves lives.
   D. Her saved their life.

9. A. The tree leafs fell on himself.
   B. The tree leaves fell on him.
   C. The tree leafs on him fell.
   D. The tree leaves fell on he.

10. A. I myself saw wolves on TV last night.
    B. I me saw wolves on TV last night.
    C. I saw myself wolves on TV last night.
    D. I saw wolves on TV last myself night.

11. A. You punish you.
    B. You punish your.
    C. You yourself punish.
    D. You punish yourself.

12. A. She baked ten loaves of bread her.
    B. She baked ten loaves of bread she.
    C. Her baked ten loaves of bread herself.
    D. She baked ten loaves of bread herself.

13. A. Mike found a thieves in his house.
    B. Mike found a thief in his house.
    C. Mike found a thief in him house.
    D. Mike found a thieves in himself house.

14. A. Mike him found the thieves.
    B. Mike himself found the thiefs.
    C. Mike he found the thieves.
    D. Mike himself found the thieves.

15. A. The wolfs cleaned their pups.
    B. The wolves cleaned their pups.
    C. The wolfs cleaned them pups.
    D. The wolves cleaned themselves pups.

16. A. The wolfs cleaned themselves pups them.
    B. The wolves themselfs cleaned their pups.
    C. The wolves cleaned pups their themselves.
    D. The wolves cleaned their pups themselves.

17. A. He liked my cake best.
    B. Him liked my cake best.
    C. He liked me cake best.
    D. He liked myself cake best.

18. A. She stood on the cliff with himself.
    B. Her stood on the cliff with he.
    C. She stood on the cliff with him.
    D. She on the cliff with him stood.

19. A. She her loved the yellow maple leaves.
    B. She herself loved yellow the maple leaves.
    C. She herself the yellow maple leaves loved.
    D. She herself loved the yellow maple leaves.

20. A. She loved herself yellow maple trees.
    B. She loved her yellow maple trees.
    C. She loved she yellow maple trees.
    D. She loved yellow her maple trees.

21. A. He feels good about himself.
    B. He feels good about themself.
    C. He good about himself feels.
    D. He feels good about his.

22. A. They believe in themselves.
    B. They believe in their self.
    C. They in themselves believe.
    D. They believe in they.

23. A. These farmers hope for rain on themselves fields.
    B. This farmers hope for rain on their fields.
    C. These farmers hope for rain on their fields.
    D. These farmers hope for rain on them fields.

24. A. She said they herself.
    B. She said it her.
    C. She said it she.
    D. She said it herself.

25. A. They loved them house.
    B. They loved themselves house.
    C. They loved their house.
    D. They loved house their.

Exercise 6.4

Sentence Building. Write the sentences in the correct order for the meaning required. Make sure the first letter of each sentence is capitalized, and the sentence ends in a period.

Emphasize who does the action:

1. Dr. Carson / book / the / himself / wrote

   ____

2. Ms. Weiss / plants / the / herself / watered

   ____

3. Todd / trees / the / himself / watered

   ____

4. Jill / cappuccino / the / herself / made

   ____

5. Kim / professor / her / herself / thanked

   ____

Emphasize that the agent completes the action without help:

1. Dr. Carson / book / the / himself / wrote

   ____

2. Ms. Weiss / plants / the / herself / watered

   ____

3. Todd / trees / the / himself / watered

   ____

4. Jill / cappuccino / the / herself / made

   ____

5. Kim / professor / her / herself / thanked

   ____

Indicate that the agent of the action is also the receiver:

1. Robert Downey Jr. / himself / thanked

   ____

2. they / themselves / to death / worked

   ____

3. cats / themselves / clean / keep

   ____

4. child / the / herself / playing baseball / hurt

   ____

5. they / themselves / like / didn't

   ____

➾ Practice saying all of the sentences with the correct stress.

Speaking Activity. In partners, have a dialogue about TV shows, movies, or music. Start your dialogue with some of the questions below. Come up with answers and more questions. Use as many demonstrative, intensive, and reflexive pronouns as you can.

1. Did you see that TV show about _______________?
2. Which TV show was most popular last year?
3. Which movies do you wish you had written yourself?
4. What is your favorite radio station?
5. What kind of music do you like?
6. What kinds of movies do you like?
7. What kinds of TV shows do you like?
8. Which awards shows do you watch?
9. Do you sing?
10. Do you play an instrument?

Reading. Andrea writes an e-mail to her grandmother, who is away on a trip to the mountains.

Dear Grandmother Willis,

Hi, Grandma! I hope you are having fun in the Montana mountains and the fishing is good. We all miss you and look forward to seeing you soon.

Carrie is excited about school tomorrow. She is going to give her first presentation herself. She is going to talk about the first time she danced at a pow wow. She's going to bring the dress you made for her and tell the class how proud she was to dress herself in it. It's going to be great!

I also promised to tell you about your favorite TV show. This week on *Castle*, Detective Beckett found her mother's killer. He was an assassin. She wanted to know who hired him to kill her mother. He passed himself off as the innocent brother of the murder victim, but he was really guilty of smuggling heroine into the United States and of killing his younger brother.

The coroner told Castle and Beckett that their murder victim was killed by the same man who killed Beckett's mother. The knife wounds were the same.

At first, they thought a gangster from another gang killed him to keep him from stopping their heroine business. Second, they thought his own gangster boss killed him to keep him from leaving their gang. Third, they found out that his older brother was smuggling heroine. They thought the older brother hired an assassin to kill his younger brother. Finally, they found out that the older brother himself was the assassin.

Beckett and Castle accused him of the murder. Then the murderer disarmed his guard and took Castle hostage. The police chief aimed his gun at the killer, but Beckett asked the chief to lower his gun. She wanted the killer alive. She wanted to ask him later who paid him to kill her mother. Then Castle knocked the killer in the nose with the back of his head. The killer stepped back, and Castle was free. The killer's nose bled red blood. The killer aimed his gun at the police chief. Finally, Detective Beckett shot him in the chest. She wanted him alive, but he died.

Castle felt guilty that Beckett had no chance to ask the killer who paid him to kill her mother. Nevertheless, Beckett told Castle not to blame himself: they would find the person who paid for her mother's murder together.

I hope you bring back many fish for us, Grandmother!

Love,
Andrea

Comprehension Activity.

1. Where is Grandmother Willis?

   A. She is at the beach.
   B. She is in the park.
   C. She is in the mountains.
   D. She is at the store.

2. What is Carrie going to do at school tomorrow?

   A. She is going to take a test.
   B. She is going to dance in her new dress.
   C. She is going to give a presentation.
   D. She is going to write a letter to her grandmother.

3. What is the name of grandmother's favorite TV show?

   A. Her favorite TV show is *Glee.*
   B. Her favorite TV show is *Lost.*
   C. Her favorite TV show is *Flash Forward.*
   D. Her favorite TV show is *Castle.*

4. Who is the killer?

   A. The killer is the police chief.
   B. The killer is the older brother of the victim.
   C. The killer is Castle.
   D. The killer is the coroner.

5. Who did Beckett think was the killer second?

   A. Beckett thought it was a gangster from another gang.
   B. Beckett thought it was the older brother.
   C. Beckett thought it was her mother.
   D. Beckett thought it was the victim's gangster boss.

6. What did the killer do first when Beckett accused him?

   A. The killer took Castle hostage.
   B. The killer disarmed his guard.
   C. The killer shot the police chief.
   D. The killer stepped back.

7. Why did Beckett ask the police chief to lower his gun?

   A. She wanted to ask the killer who paid him to kill her mother.
   B. She wanted the killer to escape.
   C. She wanted to shoot the killer herself.
   D. She wanted Castle to shoot the killer.

8. What did Castle do to make the killer let him free?

   A. Castle paid him.
   B. Castle stepped on his toes.
   C. Castle hit him in the nose.
   D. Castle asked him to let him go.

9. Why did Castle feel guilty?

   A. Castle killed Beckett's mother himself.
   B. Castle let the killer take him hostage.
   C. Castle paid the killer to murder Beckett's mother.
   D. Castle let the killer die before saying who paid him.

✎ **Writing Activity.** Write an e-mail to a relative or friend about a TV show or movie you saw recently. Use an informal salutation and closing line, like the ones Andrea uses to her grandmother. Organize your e-mail into separate paragraphs with separate topics, like Andrea does.

Chapter 7: Learning About Others

Grammar

Questions, Modals for Questions, Question Marks, Word Order and Tone for Questions.

Dialogue

Dialogue for pronunciation and intonation. The teacher reads to the class, emphasizing pronunciation and intonation. The teacher reads Darryl's part while students read Kim's part. Students pair up and practice the dialogue, and then switch parts and practice again. The teacher corrects pronunciation and intonation.

Darryl	Hi, Kim. Sit with me. Dr. Carson wants us to interview each other and introduce each other to the class.
Kim	OK. Are those questions on the board the ones we're supposed to ask each other?
Darryl	He said to use four or five of those, and to ask our own follow-up questions.
Kim	Oh, good. We can ask more detailed questions.
Darryl	That's right. Are you ready?
Kim	Who goes first?
Darryl	I'll start. What is your name?
Kim	My name is Kim Tapscott.
Darryl	Where were you born?
Kim	I was born in Fresno, California.
Darryl	What is your college major?
Kim	My college major is biology.
Darryl	Really? I thought it was English. You're such a good writer.
Kim	Dr. Jones says biologists need to write too.
Darryl	I'll make a note of it. What year are you in college?
Kim	I'm in my third year; I'm a junior.
Darryl	You're a year ahead of me! I'm a sophomore.
Kim	I'm sorry.
Darryl	Ha ha. OK. Tell me about your family. Do you have any brothers or sisters?

Kim	I have a twin brother Tim, and we live with our parents here in town.
Darryl	I had a class with Tim last year. Nice guy. Does he ever talk?
Kim	He mostly studies. He's a very serious student. I like to think we both are.
Darryl	Yeah, OK. What are your career goals?
Kim	I love English and biology. I want to be a science writer.
Darryl	A science writer? Are there any science writers who inspire you?
Kim	Oh, yeah. Charles Darwin and Rachel Carson. I also love *Scientific American* and *Discover* magazine. I like to study in the coffee shop in the Barnes & Noble bookstore. I scour the science magazines when I can.
Darryl	Wow, that's impressive. I didn't know your tastes were so refined.
Kim	I'm not sure if that's a compliment or an insult.
Darryl	A compliment, I assure you. I should start going to Barnes & Noble.
Kim	As long as you're there to read. May I ask the questions now?
Darryl	Please, go ahead.
Kim	OK. What is your name?
Darryl	My name is Darryl Lafayette.
Kim	That's a nice name.
Darryl	I'm glad you like it.
Kim	All right, where are you from?
Darryl	I was born in New Orleans, Louisiana.
Kim	No way! Really?
Darryl	Really, but my parents moved here before Hurricane Katrina. We used to live in the French Quarter.
Kim	Oh! That's amazing! I am so jealous! When did you move to California?
Darryl	We moved here ten years ago.
Kim	Why did your family move here?
Darryl	My parents work in solar technology. Their company moved here.
Kim	Well, Fresno gets a lot of sun. What is your college major?
Darryl	My major is music.
Kim	Do you play an instrument?
Darryl	I play a few instruments.
Kim	Really? Which ones?
Darryl	My favorite instrument to play is the trumpet, but I also like playing the tenor saxophone.
Kim	Where can I hear you play?
Darryl	There's a club downtown. I'll let you know about our next gig. You can bring your brother and your friends.

Kim I will. Let me know. What's your cell phone number?

Darryl That question isn't on the board.

Kim It's a follow-up question.

Darryl Fair enough. Nine-seven-zero, two-four-three-one.

Kim How did you know you wanted to play music?

Darryl An old man lived next door to us in New Orleans. My family kind of looked after him. He had vinyl records and an old record player. He played those scratchy old records every afternoon. I couldn't wait to get out of school and go visit him. We'd listen to Count Basie and Miles Davis.

Kim I can see you as a kid, sitting on the porch and listening to records. Do you have any brothers or sisters?

Darryl I have three sisters: Danielle, Donna, and Daria.

Kim How old are they?

Darryl They're all older than me. I'm twenty. Danielle is the oldest; she is thirty, married with a family and living in Atlanta, Georgia. She's a realtor. Donna is twenty-seven. She's in Los Angeles. She's fluent in Spanish and does Spanish-language advertising. Daria is twenty-two. She is here at the university, majoring in English. She wants to teach English as a second language in the public schools, but she is also thinking about teaching English abroad.

Kim Wow, your family's really interesting. I guess I won't get to meet them, though.

Darryl My parents are here, and everybody comes back here for Christmas.

Kim I think we have enough for our introductions. I like this assignment. It's a great way to start the semester.

Darryl Yeah, it is.

Vocabulary

✓ Nouns

advertising
afternoon
assignment
board
bookstore
career goals
Christmas
club
college major
company
compliment
downtown

French Quarter
friend
gig
guy
instrument
insult
introduction
magazine
name
neighborhood
porch
public school
questions
realtor
record player
saxophone
science writer
semester
solar technology
sun
tastes
trumpet
twin
vinyl record
way

✐ Verbs

assure
inspire
interview
introduce
listen
look after
meet
miss
scour
supposed
visit
wait

✐ Adjectives

abroad
amazing
born
detailed
enough
favorite
first
impressive
interesting
next
ready
refined
scratchy

Questions. All questions begin with a capital letter and end with a question mark (?). There are different types of questions: closed questions, polite requests, and open questions.

Closed Questions are answered "yes" or "no." Yes / no questions begin with the "to be" verb or the "to do" verb.

- *Is* that your saxophone?
- *Are* those the questions?
- *Am* I on time?
- *Were* they in solar technology?

When the closed question uses a "to be" verb, then the verb moves to the first position in the sentence, and the subject to the second position. Compare the word order in the questions above with the word order in the statements below:

- That *is* your saxophone.
- Those *are* the questions.
- I *am* on time.
- They *were* in solar technology.

Closed questions usually have rising intonation. This means that the pitch or stress rises toward the end of the question. Statements, polite requests, and open questions usually have falling intonation, which means that the pitch or stress becomes less toward the end of the sentence. Practice asking the closed questions with rising intonation. Practice saying the statements with falling intonation.

When "to be" is not the main verb, *do / does / did* goes in the first position as a helping verb, and the main verb follows the subject. Note also that the "do" verb agrees with the subject of the sentence, and the main verb takes the base form: "Does he want," not "Does he wants."

- Do you *have* brothers or sisters?
- Do we *need* more time?
- Does he *want* us to interview each other?
- Does she *like* the assignment?

Compare the word order and verb form in the questions above with statements here:

- You *have* brothers or sisters.
- We *need* more time.
- He *wants* us to interview each other.
- She *likes* the assignment.

Practice asking the closed questions with rising intonation. Practice saying the statements with falling intonation.

Polite Requests have the same word order as the yes / no questions above, but they do not begin with *do*. They begin with a helping verb such as *can, may, could,* or *would,* and the main verb takes the base form. Some polite requests ask for permission to do something. They begin with *May* or *Can*.

- *May* I ask the questions now?
- *May* we sit with you?
- *Can* I get your cell phone number?
- *Can* he have a slice of pizza?
- *Can* she go to the store now?

Practice asking the polite requests using falling intonation.

Some polite questions are an offer to do something for someone else. They begin with *Should I, Can I,* or *Would you like.*

- *Should* I open the door for you?
- *Can* I carry your bags for you?
- *Should* I get you a plate?
- *Can* I get you a mocha frappuccino?
- *Would* you like a pastry?

Practice asking the polite requests using falling intonation.

Other polite questions ask the person you are addressing to do something for you. They begin with *Could you* or *Would you.*

- *Could* you open the door for me?
- *Would* you tell me the time?
- *Could* you tell me what the assignment is?
- *Would* you show me where the craft store is?

Practice asking the polite requests using falling intonation.

Open Questions are answered with information, not just yes or no. They begin with *who, whose, what, which, when, where, why,* or *how.*

- *Who* is your brother?
- *Whose* saxophone is that?
- *What* does he want us to do?
- *Which* instruments do you play?
- *When* should I arrive?

- *Where* do you live?
- *Why* do you want to be a science writer?
- *How* did you study for the midterm?

These questions require information: a name, an activity, a list of items, a time, a location, a reason, and a way of doing something. They cannot be answered with a simple yes or no. Practice asking the open questions using falling intonation.

Exercise 7.1

Multiple choice. Circle the letter in front of the sentence with the correct word order for a question.

1. A. Do you like English?
   B. Like you English?
   C. Do you English like?
   D. You do like English?

2. A. That is your backpack?
   B. Is that your backpack?
   C. That your backpack is?
   D. Do that backpack is your?

3. A. They did go to the university?
   B. Go they to the university did?
   C. Did they to the university go?
   D. Did they go to the university?

4. A. You are ready for class?
   B. You ready for class are?
   C. Are you ready for class?
   D. Do you for class are ready?

5. A. Who has a question?
   B. Has who a question?
   C. Who a question has?
   D. A question who has?

6. A. Where is your class?
   B. Is where your class?
   C. Is your class where?
   D. Where your class is?

7. A. What your name is?
   B. Is your name what?
   C. Your name is what?
   D. What is your name?

8. A. Does when the semester begin?
   B. When does the semester begin?
   C. When begin the semester does?
   D. When the semester does begin?

9. A. Is where your cell phone?
   B. Where is your cell phone?
   C. Your cell phone is where?
   D. Where your cell phone is?

10. A. Did choose you why that college major?
    B. Why you did choose that college major?
    C. Choose did you why that college major?
    D. Why did you choose that college major?

11. A. Whose book this is?
    B. Book whose is this?
    C. Whose book is this?
    D. Whose is this book?

12. A. Could I you a pen get?
    B. I could get you a pen?
    C. Could I get you a pen?
    D. I you a pen could get?

13. A. Would you like some paper?
    B. Would some paper like you?
    C. Would you some paper like?
    D. You some paper would like?

14. A. I your class notes may read?
    B. May I your class notes read?
    C. May I read your class notes?
    D. Your class notes may I read?

15. A. You would join our group?
B. Would you our group join?
C. Would you join our group?
D. You our group would join?

16. A. Can I a pen borrow?
B. Can I borrow a pen?
C. I a pen can borrow?
D. Borrow can I a pen?

17. A. What day this is?
B. What is day this?
C. This day what is?
D. What day is this?

18. A. Who to class late came?
B. Who to class came late?
C. Came to class who late?
D. Who came to class late?

19. A. When are you going to San Francisco?
B. When to San Francisco are you going?
C. To San Francisco when are you going?
D. When going to San Francisco are you?

20. A. Is where the Golden Gate Bridge?
B. Where is the Golden Gate Bridge?
C. Where the Golden Gate Bridge is?
D. Is the Golden Gate Bridge where?

21. A. Where Dr. Carson's office is?
B. Where office Dr. Carson's is?
C. Where is Dr. Carson's office?
D. Is where Dr. Carson's office?

22. A. How an A did I get on my exam?
B. How an A on my exam did I get?
C. An A on my exam how did I get?
D. How did I get an A on my exam?

23. A. Caught up are you with your class work?
B. Caught up with your class work are you?
C. You caught up are with your class work?
D. Are you caught up with your class work?

24. A. You the assignment do like?
    B. Do you the assignment like?
    C. Do you like the assignment?
    D. Do the assignment you like?

25. A. Which did he take class last semester?
    B. Which class did he take last semester?
    C. Did he take which class last semester?
    D. Did he which class last semester take?

Exercise 7.2

Sentence Building. Put the following questions in the correct word order. Questions begin with a capital letter and end with a question mark.

1. Tim / test / the / did / take

   ____

2. Tim / test / which / did / take

   ____

3. Darryl / office / Dr. Carson's / to / did / go

   ____

4. I / quiz / a / could / have

   ____

5. Kim / backpack / her / where / did / get

   ____

6. desk / your / this / is

   ____

7. I / with / you / could / sit

   ____

8. you / keys / your / how / did / find

   ____

9. they / asking / what / are

____

10. you / class / on Friday / do / have

____

11. you / pen / a / would / like

____

12. who / score / the / highest / got / on the test

____

13. professor / your / who / is / biology / for

____

14. I / window / a / could / open

____

15. bicycle / whose / that / is

____

16. you / class notes / my / would / like to see

____

17. I / late / am

____

18. I / test score / my / could / see

____

19. you / absent / were

____

20. Kim / homework / her / does / have

____

21. Darryl / paper / his / did / finish

____

22. you / when / absent / were

____

23. you / weekend / last / what / did / do

____

24. you / beach / the / did / go to

____

25. I / dog / your / could / pet

____

26. he / dogs / does / like

____

27. I / you / a cup of coffee / a / could / get

____

28. papers / the / where / are

____

29. papers / the / good / were

____

30. you / paper / your / did / like

____

➩ Practice asking the questions using rising intonation for closed questions, and falling intonation for open questions and polite requests.

Speaking Activity. Write a list of questions for interviewing your partner in class. Ask questions about your partner's

- name
- place of birth
- current city of residence
- brothers and sisters
- major and year in college
- career goals and reasons for studying English

Ask follow-up questions as you think of them. Practice several times asking and answering the questions with your partner. Be sure to use the correct intonation. Be prepared to perform your interview for the class. That is, you will take turns interviewing each other in front of the class.

Reading. Below is an e-mail from a college student to a professor asking questions about the course he is enrolled in.

Dear Dr. Carson:

I am Darryl Lafayette, a student in your two o'clock Tuesday-Thursday African American literature class. The class was really full yesterday, and I did not get a syllabus. I have a few questions for you.

- Could I stop by your office later and pick up a couple of syllabuses for me and my friend?
- Where is your office?
- When are your office hours?
- Are all the books for the class in the bookstore today?
- Do you accept late papers?
- Can I turn in my work early if I know I will be absent?
- Are we going to do library research for our papers?
- Could I do my class presentation on the poet Langston Hughes?

I am only planning to miss one week of class. I am a music major, and the jazz band has some concerts scheduled for the week of October 5th. I'm playing a saxophone solo also. This is why I am asking about missing classes, and about doing my presentation on Langston Hughes. He was influenced by jazz music, and I want to look at the effects on his poetry.

My sister Daria raves about how much she loved your class. You influenced her to be an English major. I really love literature even though I am not an English major. I am thinking about minoring in African American studies, and I hope you can advise me about this sometime later on.

Sincerely,
Darryl Lafayette

Comprehension Activity

1. What class is Darryl taking?
2. When is he taking it?
3. Who is he taking it from?
4. What does he want to pick up at his professor's office?
5. Does Darryl know where Dr. Carson's office is?
6. Why is Darryl asking about turning in late papers?
7. What kind of band does Darryl play in?
8. Which poet was influenced by jazz music?
9. Who influenced Daria to become an English major?
10. What college subject does Darryl want to minor in?

Writing Activity. Carefully read the syllabus for this class. Make a note of the information in the syllabus. Think about what you would like to know that is not stated in the syllabus.

Write an e-mail to your professor in which you ask questions about your class. Three of your questions can be answered on the syllabus. Ask three more questions that are not answered on the syllabus.

Follow the format used by Darryl.

Chapter 8: Working at Macy's

Grammar

Prepositions and Word Order in Prepositional Phrases.

Dialogue

Dialogue for pronunciation and intonation. The teacher reads to the class, emphasizing pronunciation and intonation. The teacher reads John's part while students read Dave's part. Students pair up and practice the dialogue, and then switch parts and practice again. The teacher corrects pronunciation and intonation.

John Good morning, Dave. How are you?

Dave I'm fine, John. How are you?

John I'm good. It looks like we're going to get those new cashmere sweaters by Friday.

Dave Great. I'm going to get the sales items onto the display tables and make a place for the new shipment.

John Thanks, Dave. Could you also straighten up the silk ties? We had a lot of customers in the store yesterday, and I think it's a bit messy over there.

Dave Sure, OK. Hey, John, did you see my application for assistant manager in the men's clothing department?

John Yes, you got it in on time. Good luck with it.

Dave Thanks. I think the display tables should be right in front of the main doors. Customers could find what they want more easily, and less of the store would get messy.

John That's good thinking, Dave. That would cut our workload and allow us to cut some part-time employees. Still, I think the company wants customers to look around in the store. They buy more clothes when they see more clothes.

Dave Ah. That's what executives are for: figuring out how to get customers to spend more money.

John It's a living. I almost forgot! Those jeans you wanted came in last night. They're in boxes in the back. We can take them out after we straighten up this place.

Dave That's great! I guess I should also straighten up the shelves along the wall.

John Uh, yeah, that would be good. Let me give you a hand. I don't have to open the doors for another twenty minutes.

Dave OK. Could you straighten up the silk ties while I arrange the display tables?

John Yeah. Dave?

Dave Yes?

John I was thinking about your idea for training new employees.

Dave Yeah.

John New employees do need more training on the register and in customer service. The other day I caught Terry telling Henry Hernandez that we couldn't get the hat he wanted. Terry was a little rude about it. I pulled Terry aside afterward and explained to him that we don't treat regular customers like that. I special ordered Henry's hat, and paid for the shipping myself. I was embarrassed.

Dave I heard about that. Unfortunately, I don't think Terry understood what he did wrong.

John Terry needs to learn. I can replace him tomorrow. I have a file drawer full of applications. Uh, please don't tell anyone I said that to you.

Dave Terry deserves it. He's rude to all the male customers. He's rude to everyone who isn't a pretty woman, actually.

John Hm. That's got to stop. This is a men's department. Still, Terry is a perfect example of our problem. We can fire all the rude sales clerks and hire new people tomorrow. Or, we can train them to be better sales clerks.

Dave That's what I was thinking. I'm finished over here.

John If we start fresh with new employees, we still have to train them to do the register, know what we have in stock and on sale, and talk nicely to people. I mean, there's no reason to assume the ones we hire fresh will be any better than Terry. Indeed, they may be very much worse. Terry is reliable. He is always on time and never misses a day of work. That's always good for business.

Dave We could put sales staff into teams with a more experienced leader. They can have a meeting every week or two to talk about problems. Let them talk freely about what's bothering them in order to build trust within the teams. Senior staff can schedule each meeting around one lesson. The senior staff can lead the lesson. When they're done, they can let the junior staff lead discussion.

John The cost of your plan is only more employee hours. I think the older staff would like the recognition. I can see it working. Did you get this idea from one of your college classes?
Dave Actually, I did. Dr. An taught us this in English composition.
John Wow. I guess general education does have its benefits. Time to open the doors!

Vocabulary

✓ Nouns

application
assistant manager
benefit
cashmere sweaters
clothes
cost
customer service
department
discussion
display table
employee hours
example
executives
file drawer
Friday
general education
idea
jeans
lesson
luck
main doors
male
men's clothing
part-time employee
sale
sales clerk
shelves
shipment
silk tie
staff
stock
tomorrow
training
trust
understanding
wall
workload
yesterday

✓ Verbs

allow
arrange
assume
build
catch
deserve
explain
figure out
fire
give you / me a hand
looks like
miss (work)
open
order

pull aside
schedule
stop
straighten up
supervise
teach
train
treat

✐ Adjectives

a bit
a lot
embarrassed
experienced
finished
fresh
full
messy
perfect
pretty
reliable
rude
regular
wrong
younger

Prepositions describe location or direction. English has had prepositions for over a millennium, but Old English has fewer than Modern English. Like many ancient languages, Old English has a case system: nouns have endings that give information similar to the prepositions. Over time, English lost most of its cases: only the possessive and pronoun cases remain. So, prepositions take the place of cases. As a result, Modern English speakers expect to hear and read prepositions that give specific information about location, direction, and other types of relationships.

✐ Prepositions

about
around
by
for
from
in
into
of
on
onto
over
to
with
within

The original and concrete use of prepositions is to mark where something is in space, or where it is going to or leaving from. Practice saying the list of prepositions.

Look at the image of the plastic cup below. Note that specific prepositions indicate a specific spatial relationship to the cup. Also, notice the prepositional phrases that describe these relationships.

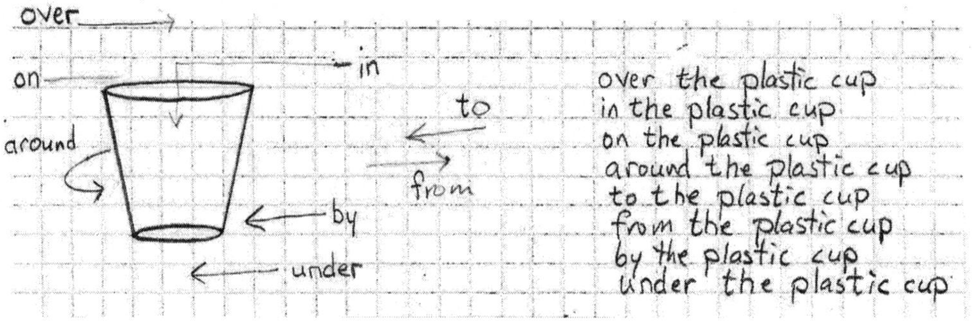

As you review the dialogue, you find that some of these prepositions, such as "about," now also describe abstract relationships. You can *walk about the house*, but you can also *talk about movies*. The first use indicates concrete, physical movement. The second indicates abstract movement.

For in-class discussion, review the dialogue between John and Dave in this chapter and discuss which prepositions are concrete, and which abstract. Also discuss what the prepositions mean.

Word Order for Prepositional Phrases. The preposition comes first in a prepositional phrase. Prepositions are followed by nouns, pronouns, or noun phrases. The word order for noun phrases is 1) article or demonstrative or possessive pronoun; 2) adjective; and 3) noun.

onto the table	*under the light*	*about the house*
at their store	*in her car*	*on the bus*
around the park	*by his sister*	*within the group*
over the hill	*into the bag*	*from the store*
for her uncle	*of the children*	*with his friends*

The stress in a prepositional phrase falls on the noun at the end. Practice saying the prepositional phrases.

🔍 Irregular verbs in which the past tense ends in "ught."

Present tense	Past tense	Pronunciation
bring	brought	/ ȯ /
buy	bought	/ ȯ /
catch	caught	/ ȯ /
fight	fought	/ ȯ /
teach	taught	/ ȯ /
think	thought	/ ȯ /

➾ Practice saying the words in the present and past tenses.

Exercise 8.1

Multiple choice. Circle the letter in front of the sentence with the correct word order.

1. A. John brought Henry to the party.
   B. John Henry to the party brought.
   C. John brought Henry the party to.
   D. John brought Henry party the to.

2. A. Dave a coat for his mother bought.
   B. Dave bought a coat his mother for.
   C. Dave bought a coat for his mother.
   D. Dave bought coat a mother his for.

3. A. John about the store walked.
   B. John walked about the store.
   C. John walked the store about.
   D. John walked store the about.

4. A. Dave shelves over his bed built.
   B. Dave shelves built over his bed.
   C. Dave built shelves his bed over.
   D. Dave built shelves over his bed.

5. A. Sally walked house Todd's to.
   B. Sally walked to Todd's house.
   C. Sally to Todd's house walked.
   D. Sally walked Todd's house to.

6. A. Mr. Hernandez worked house the around.
   B. Mr. Hernandez worked around the house.
   C. Mr. Hernandez around the house worked.
   D. Mr. Hernandez house the around worked.

7. A. Terry works in the men's department.
   B. Terry works the in men's department.
   C. Terry in the men's department works.
   D. Terry works in the department men's.

8. A. Andrea put the tamales on the table.
   B. Andrea put the tamales the table on.
   C. Andrea put the tamales table the on.
   D. Andrea the tamales on the table put.

9. A. Dr. Mike Carson lives the Hernandez family by.
   B. Dr. Mike Carson by the Hernandez family lives.
   C. Dr. Mike Carson lives by the Hernandez family.
   D. Dr. Mike Carson lives family the Hernandez by.

10. A. We can keep this story you and me between.
    B. We can keep this story between you and me.
    C. We can this story between you and me keep.
    D. We can keep you and me this story between.

11. A. The bird felt safe within its flock.
    B. The bird safe within its flock felt.
    C. The bird felt safe flock its within.
    D. The bird felt safe its within flock.

12. A. Henry got his hat Macy's from.
    B. Henry his hat got from Macy's.
    C. Henry got his hat from Macy's.
    D. Henry his hat Macy's from got.

13. A. Dr. Jones in class is.
    B. Dr. Jones is in class.
    C. Dr. Jones in is class.
    D. Class is in Dr. Jones.

14. A. Dr. Carson is office in his.
    B. Office Dr. Carson is his in.
    C. Dr. Carson in his office is.
    D. Dr. Carson is in his office.

15. A. Ms. Weiss is cell phone her on.
    B. Ms. Weiss is her cell phone on.
    C. Ms. Weiss on her cell phone is.
    D. Ms. Weiss is on her cell phone.

16. A. Todd went into the arboretum.
    B. Todd went arboretum the into.
    C. Todd went the arboretum into.
    D. Todd into the arboretum went.

17. A. Jill works at Starbucks with Andrea.
    B. Jill works at Starbucks Andrea with.
    C. Jill works Starbucks at with Andrea.
    D. Jill at Starbucks with Andrea works.

18. A. Dr. Sang-hee An ran the hill over.
    B. Dr. Sang-hee An ran hill the over.
    C. Dr. Sang-hee An ran over the hill.
    D. Dr. Sang-hee An over the hill ran.

19. A. Mike walked across the bridge.
    B. Mike walked the bridge across.
    C. Mike walked across bridge the.
    D. Mike across the bridge walked.

20. A. Dave work on Thursday missed.
    B. Dave missed work Thursday on.
    C. Dave missed work on Thursday.
    D. Dave missed Thursday work on.

21. A. John Terry on the phone at work caught.
    B. John caught Terry on the phone at work.
    C. John caught Terry the phone on work at.
    D. John caught Terry on phone the at work.

22. A. Henry Terry over a hat fought.
    B. Henry fought Terry a hat over.
    C. Henry fought Terry hat a over.
    D. Henry fought Terry over a hat.

23. A. Emma rode in Henry's car.
    B. Emma rode car Henry's in.
    C. Emma rode Henry's in car.
    D. Emma in Henry's car rode.

24. A. I got the airplane on with you.
    B. I got on airplane the you with.
    C. I got on the airplane with you.
    D. I on the airplane with you got.

25. A. You with me got in the car.
    B. You got with me the in car.
    C. You got in the car with me.
    D. You in the car me with got.

Exercise 8.2

Sentence Building. Write a meaningful sentence, with the correct word order, for each of the groups of words below. Sentences begin with a capital letter and end with a period.

1. Emma / cashmere sweater / a / Uncle Tomás / bought / for

   ____

2. Tim / father / his / fought / with

   ____

3. sales clerk / that / customers / our / rude / was / to

   ____

4. Dave / application / his / desk / John's / on / put

   ____

5. Henry / wall / the / around / walked

   ____

6. Andrea / tamales / the / bag / the / into / put

   ____

7. Andrea / pork / the / sandwiches / the / into / put

   ____

8. John / himself / store / the / in / embarrassed

____

9. John / application / the / file drawer / the / out of / took

____

10. Mr. Hernandez / silk tie / a / restaurant / the / to / wore

____

11. shipment / the / Friday / on / came

____

12. she / classes / her / Wednesday / for / scheduled

____

13. he / soup / dinner / for / ordered

____

14. they / work / to / go / today

____

15. they / work / to / went / yesterday

____

16. Dr. Carson / poems / a lot / of / taught

____

17. John / Terry / tip / a / gave

____

18. he / men's clothing / in / worked

____

19. assistant manager / the / main doors / the / through / walked

____

20. lesson / the / in Chinese / was

____

21. examples / those / board / the / on / are

____

22. dog / the / park / the / across / runs

____

23. book / the / Dr. Carson / by / was written

____

24. Tim / exam / the / through / read

____

25. Kim / exam / the / over / read

____

➾ Practice saying the sentences with the correct intonation.

Speaking Activity. With a partner, pretend you are shopping together in a clothing store. First, practice saying the phrases below. Then, write a dialogue with your partner and read it for the class.

✐ Clothing

shoes	underwear	hats
boots	bras	scarves
shirts	stockings	gloves
pants	socks	sweaters
ties	pajamas	coats

✐ Example Prepositional Phrases

bought those shoes *for his sister*
matched this sweater *with that shirt*
sold green scarves *to his grandmother*
tried on the pants *in the store*
wore his pajamas *to bed*
got his hat *at Macy's*
went to the store *for socks*

➾ Practice saying the phrases with the correct intonation.

✓ Store Furnishings

display tables	racks	fitting room
register	hangers	doors
counter	mannequins	wall
shelves	floor	

✓ Example Prepositional Phrases

on the display tables
by the register
at the counter
on hangers
in the fitting room
below the mannequin

➾ Practice saying the phrases with the correct intonation.

Exercise 8.3

Fill in the blanks. Choose the correct one of these words for each answer: *around, by, from, in, on, over, to,* and *under.*

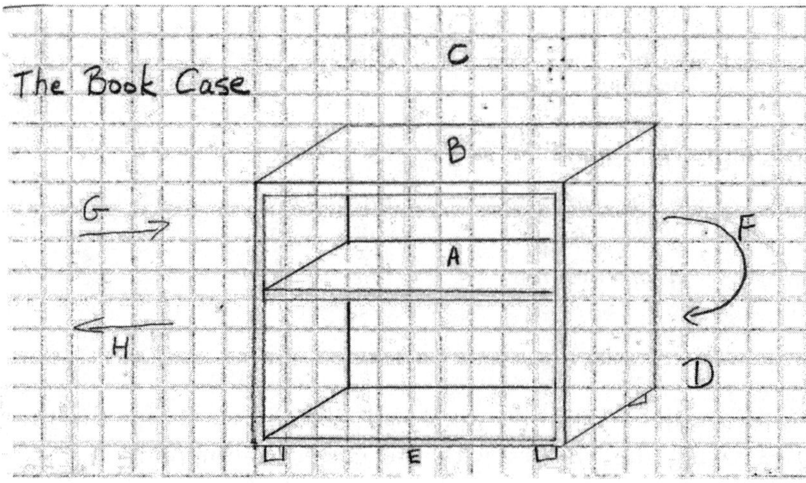

A. ____________
B. ____________
C. ____________
D. ____________
E. ____________
F. ____________
G. ____________
H. ____________

✓ Days of the Week

Sunday	Wednesday	Saturday
Monday	Thursday	
Tuesday	Friday	

✓ Example Prepositional Phrases

on Sunday	*before Tuesday*	*since Friday*
after Wednesday	*until Saturday*	*past Monday*

All of these prepositions work with all of these days of the week. Practice saying the phrases with the correct intonation.

✓ Months of the Year

January	May	September
February	June	October
March	July	November
April	August	December

✓ Example Prepositional Phrases

in January	*before April*	*at the end of July*
during February	*at the start of May*	*since August*
after March	*in the middle of June*	*until October*

All of these prepositions work with all of these months of the year. Practice saying the phrases with the correct intonation.

✓ Times of Day

dawn	afternoon	night
morning	dusk	twilight
noon	evening	

✓ Example Prepositional Phrases

at dawn	*in the morning*	*after dawn*
at noon	*in the afternoon*	*after dusk*
at dusk	*in the evening*	*after twilight*
at night		
at twilight		

These specific prepositions can only work with specific words for the times of day. Practice saying the phrases with the correct intonation.

Reading. Below is a cover letter. Dave Cho is applying for a promotion in his own store.

Dear Mr. Wright:

I am writing to apply for the position of assistant sales manager in the Men's Clothing Department at Macy's in the Sierra Nevada Mall. I have worked hard as a sales clerk at this store for four years. In addition, I have just completed my bachelors degree in business at the University of Central California with a 3.9 grade point average.

As a sales clerk, I was able to develop highly effective skills in store display, customer service, and unit leadership. In 2008, photos of my store displays were used as models at the annual Macy's conference in San Francisco. In 2009, I was recognized as employee of the month three times in the months of July, August, and December because of my conflict-management approach to customer complaints. My supervisor asked me to train new employees using the same method in 2009. In January, 2010, my peers in my department awarded me the unit leadership award. I must admit, it was my proudest day.

Macy's needs managers who can train their employees to treat customers with respect, and who can help customers choose clothing suitable to their work and life. At the University of Central California, I excelled not only in business management and accounting classes, but also in advertising and fashion courses. I have many loyal customers who come to my department because they trust my fashion sense, and my personal pledge to them not to let them leave the store unless they look their best.

Macy's is my home. It is where I grew up in the business world. I want to keep growing with Macy's. I want the job of assistant sales manager, and if I am chosen, I will make the company proud.

Sincerely yours,
David Cho

Comprehension Activity

1. Why does Dave write to Mr. Wright?
2. Where is the store Dave works at?
3. What is Dave's bachelors degree in?
4. What does Dave say about his store displays?
5. When was Dave recognized as employee of the month?
6. What award did Dave's peers give him?
7. Which classes did Dave excel in?
8. Why are Dave's customers loyal?
9. What job does Dave want?

Writing Activity. Write a cover letter to apply for a job. Choose a job in a career path you think you would enjoy. Study the content and organization in Dave's letter, and compose a letter with a similar organization and format.

Chapter 9: Taking Inventory

Grammar

Countable, Noncountable, and Collective Nouns, Nouns that are always plural (pants, scissors).

Dialogue

Dialogue for pronunciation and intonation. The teacher reads to the class, emphasizing pronunciation and intonation. The teacher reads Sally's part while students read Shirley's part. Students pair up and practice the dialogue, and then switch parts and practice again. The teacher corrects pronunciation and intonation.

Sally Good morning, Shirley.

Shirley Hi, Sally. I made coffee.

Sally Thanks, I'll have a cup of coffee. Is there any sugar?

Shirley There are packets of sugar in the cabinet.

Sally Are those your scissors on the floor?

Shirley Yes, it looks like they fell off the table. It's my favorite pair.

Sally I thought you held onto them all day.

Shirley I try to. The Wilson family came in yesterday, and it was a big group. Each one of them seemed to want my attention at the same time.

Sally Did they come in just before closing time?

Shirley Yes, but they spent a lot of money.

Sally Well, that's good. I called the distributor yesterday about the toy bears we got the other day. I think the dye may be toxic. I never held much faith in that company.

Shirley Some of them smell really strong.

Sally I hope we can send some of them back. I don't want any of our customers to complain or get sick.

Shirley Most of our customers are loyal. You won't have to worry.

Sally I want to keep their loyalty. How much coffee is left?

Shirley There's more than enough coffee for two more cups.

Sally Ah, good. Let's check the stock. How many needles do we have?

Shirley We have two hundred needles. Many of the needles are for fabric; few of the needles are for leather.

Sally How much clay do we have?

Shirley We have five kilograms of clay. Much of the clay is gray; little of the clay is red.

Sally How many skeins of yarn do we have?

Shirley We have fifty skeins of yarn. Few of the skeins are orange; many of the skeins are brown.

Sally How much tissue paper do we have?

Shirley We have twelve boxes of tissue paper. Much of the tissue paper is pink; little of it is blue.

Sally How many knitting needles do we have?

Shirley We have fifty knitting needles.

Sally I think we have enough stock for the week. How many women and men came into the store this week?

Shirley Forty women came into the store since Monday morning. Fifteen men came into the store. Seventeen children came with some of the adults.

Sally Oh no, I spilled coffee on my pants.

Shirley Here's a napkin. It's a good thing your pants are black; the stain will not show.

Sally I bought this pair of pants last month.

Shirley That is a nice pair of pants. I brought a little bread and cheese for lunch later.

Sally I brought a few cherries. I picked them myself this morning. Many of my cherry trees have ripe cherries now.

Shirley I love cherries. I bought this loaf of bread at the bakery this morning. The cheese is a sharp cheddar. Mm. I may not have the patience to wait until lunch.

Sally My advice is not to wait for lunch.

Vocabulary

✓ Verbs

complain	spill
send	worry
smell	

✓ Adjectives

black	brown
blue	gray

left
loyal
orange
pink
red
sharp
strong
toxic

✓ Countable Nouns

bear
box
cabinet
cherry
children
company
cup
customer
day
distributor
floor
kilogram
loaf
men
needle
packet
pair
skein
table
time
toy
tree
women

Most nouns in English are countable. The plural form is used when there is more than one cup or packet: for example, *two cups, five tables*, and *forty packets*.

Some English nouns are treated as noncountable nouns. The same form is used no matter how many items there are.

✓ **Noncountable Nouns**

Concrete Noncountables

air
bread
cheese
clay
coffee
dirt
fabric
gasoline
leather
paper
rice
smoke
steam
sugar
water
yarn

You can count *cups* of coffee, *loaves* of bread, *sheets* of paper, *grains* of sugar, and *sticks* of chalk, but these things themselves are noncountable in English.

✐ Groups with Similar Items:

clothing
equipment
food
fruit
furniture
garbage
makeup
money
stock

✐ Abstract Noncountables:

advice
attention
beauty
courage
faith
help
honesty
importance
information
justice
knowledge
love
loyalty
patience
peace
progress
truth

The abstractions are largely concepts or qualities. Practice saying the non-countable nouns.

Noncountable nouns are in the singular form, and they take singular verbs: *Honesty is the best policy. This is good advice.*

✐ Indefinite / Comparative Pronouns with Noncountable Nouns

all	little	much
any	more	some
less	most	

- *There was much smoke.*
- *Little dirt is there.*
- *Much furniture is inside*
- *Little knowledge is needed.*

"Much" and "little" are used with noncountable nouns.

✐ Indefinite / Comparative Pronouns with Countable Nouns

all	few	many
any	more	some
fewer	most	

"Many" and "few" are used with countable nouns.

- *There were many leaves.*
- *Few American men wear pink.*
- *Many chairs are inside.*
- *Few facts are known.*

➾ Practice saying the sentences.

Exercise 9.1

Multiple choice. Circle the letter in front of the correct sentence with regard to quantity, not size.

1. A. She had two waters.
   B. She had two glasses of water.
   C. She had two water.
   D. She had two glass of water.

2. A. There were many clays on the table.
   B. There were many clay on the table.
   C. There was much clay on the table.
   D. There was much clays on the table.

3. A. He ate so much rice.
   B. He ate so many rice.
   C. He ate so much rices.
   D. He ate so many rices.

4. A. She saved few cheese for later.
   B. She saved little cheese for later.
   C. She saved few cheeses for later.
   D. She saved little cheeses for later.

5. A. They found few chalks on the street the next day.
   B. They found few chalk on the street the next day.
   C. They found less chalk on the street the next day.
   D. They found less chalks on the street the next day.

6. A. She made many money in her store.
   B. She made much money in her store.
   C. She made many moneys in her store.
   D. She made much moneys in her store.

7. A. We bought few clothing at that store.
   B. We bought little clothing at that store.
   C. We bought little clothings at that store.
   D. We bought few clothings at that store.

8. A. We found little of the stock useful.
   B. We found few of the stock useful.
   C. We found little of the stocks useful.
   D. We found few of the stocks useful.

9. A. She wore little makeups.
   B. She wore few makeup.
   C. She wore few makeups.
   D. She wore little makeup.

10. A. There was much garbages on the street.
    B. There were many garbage on the street.
    C. There was much garbage on the street.
    D. There was many garbages on the street.

11. A. His words showed much courage.
    B. His words showed many courages.
    C. His words showed much courages.
    D. His words showed many courage.

12. A. She has little faith in him.
    B. She has few faiths in him.
    C. She has few faith in him.
    D. She has little faiths in him.

13. A. The dog has many loves for Mike.
    B. The dog has many love for Mike.
    C. The dog has much loves for Mike.
    D. The dog has much love for Mike.

14. A. There was much justices in the law.
    B. There was much justice in the law.
    C. There was many justices in the law.
    D. There was many justice in the law.

15. A. This class is making much progresses.
    B. This class is making much progress.
    C. This class is making many progress.
    D. This class is making many progresses.

16. A. Show me a few honesties.
    B. Show me a few honesty.
    C. Show me a little honesty.
    D. Show me a little honesties.

17. A. The professor gave me much helps.
    B. The professor gave me many helps.
    C. The professor gave me much help.
    D. The professor gave me many help.

18. A. She had few patiences for the sales clerk.
    B. She had few patience for the sales clerk.
    C. She had little patience for the sales clerk.
    D. She had little patiences for the sales clerk.

19. A. There is less peace in the world than last year.
    B. There is less peaces in the world than last year.
    C. There are few peace in the world than last year.
    D. There are few peaces in the world than last year.

20. A. I have many faiths in you.
    B. I have many faith in you.
    C. I have much faiths in you.
    D. I have much faith in you.

21. A. There is much beauty in this park.
    B. There is much beauties in this park.
    C. There are many beauty in this park.
    D. There are many beauties in this park.

22. A. His idea was of many importances to the group.
    B. His idea was of much importance to the group.
    C. His idea was of much importances to the group.
    D. His idea was of many importance to the group.

23. A. Kim gave many attentions to Dr. Jones's lecture.
    B. Kim gave much attentions to Dr. Jones's lecture.
    C. Kim gave much attention to Dr. Jones's lecture.
    D. Kim gave many attention to Dr. Jones's lecture.

24. A. There is few love in this house.
    B. There is little love in this house.
    C. There are little loves in this house.
    D. There are few loves in this house.

25. A. There were many honesties in his words.
B. There was much honesty in his words.
C. There were much honesties in his words.
D. There is many honesty in his words.

Exercise 9.2

Fill in. Write the correct word with regard to quantity in the blank.

1. There were ___________ customers in the store.
(few / little)

2. Mrs. Hernandez bought ___________ rice at the grocery store.
(many / much)

3. Sally found ___________ boxes of buttons in the craft store.
(few / little)

4. How ___________ help do you need?
(many / much)

5. Darryl paid ___________ attention in class.
(many / much)

6. How ___________ dogs are in the park?
(many / much)

7. The actor wears ___________ makeup for the stage.
(many / much)

8. Kim saw ___________ garbage after they started recycling.
(few / less)

9. Andrea never saw so ___________ sand before.
(many / much)

10. They wanted ___________ children.
(few / little)

➾ Practice saying the sentences.

A third type of noun is the collective noun.

✓ Collective Nouns

audience	faculty	staff
class	family	team
committee	group	crowd

Collective nouns in American English usually take a singular verb and a singular pronoun:

- *That is not our group. It is Tim's group.*
- *The department faculty is too small. It has only ten professors.*
- *My family buys bread at the bakery.*

⇒ Practice saying the sentences.

Note that when the collective noun is the object of the preposition, the verb must agree with the subject of the sentence.

- Much of the audience falls asleep during the show.
- Many in the audience fall asleep during the show.

Exercise 9.3

Multiple choice. Circle the letter in front of the correct sentence.

1. A. This is a tough audience.
   B. These are a tough audience.
   C. This is a tough audiences.
   D. This are tough audiences.

2. A. Our department have strong faculties.
   B. Our department has strong faculties.
   C. Our department have a strong faculty.
   D. Our department has a strong faculty.

3. A. This group work well together.
   B. This group works well together.
   C. These group work well together.
   D. These groups works well together.

4. A. The staff likes your idea.
   B. The staff like your idea.
   C. The staffs like your idea.
   D. The staffs likes your idea.

5. A. His groups cheers each other on.
   B. His groups cheer each other on.
   C. His group cheer each other on.
   D. His group cheers each other on.

6. A. The committee likes to leave early.
   B. These committees likes to leave early.
   C. These committee like to leave early.
   D. The committee like to leave early.

7. A. These Hernandez family have pizza on Fridays.
   B. The Hernandez family have pizza on Fridays.
   C. The Hernandez family has pizza on Fridays.
   D. The Hernandez families has pizza on Fridays.

8. A. The Wilson family are happy.
   B. The Wilson family is happy.
   C. These Wilson families is happy.
   D. The Wilson families is happy.

9. A. The audience clap for the actor.
   B. The audiences clap for the actor.
   C. The audiences claps for the actor.
   D. The audience claps for the actor.

10. A. These are a good class.
    B. This is a good class.
    C. This is a good classes.
    D. These is a good class.

Exercise 9.4

Fill in. Write the correct word in the blank.

1. The staff __________ working with Dr. Carson.
   (like / likes)

2. ________ this your committee?
   (Are / Is)

3. Their team __________ the game.
   (win / wins)

4. __________ of the audience laughs at the joke.
   (Many / Much)

5. Few of the faculty ______ happy.
   (are / is)

6. The team ______ working on the project.
   (are / is)

7. __________ the staff want a longer vacation?
   (Do / Does)

8. The staff _______ large.
   (are / is)

9. How large ________ the audience?
   (are / is)

10. How many of the faculty _____________ us?
    (supports / support)

Objects with two parts are always plural.

✐ Nouns that Are Always Plural

scissors / z /	glasses / əz /	jeans / z /
pliers / z /	pants / s /	boxers / z /
shears / z /	trousers / z /	underpants / s /

Note that when "pair of" comes before any of them, they take a singular verb. For example, "The new pair of jeans *is* on the mannequin,"and "The pair of scissors is on the floor." The "s" is unvoiced (/ s /) when it follows unvoiced consonants like / t / ; the "s" is voiced (/ z /) when it follows voiced consonants like / d / and vowels. Practice saying these nouns using the correct pronunciation.

Exercise 9.5

Multiple choice. Circle the letter in front of the correct sentence.

1. A. Can you give me the scissor?
   B. Can you give me the scissors?
   C. Can you give me a scissors?
   D. Can you give me a scissor?

2. A. I need the plier.
   B. I need the pliers.
   C. I need a pliers.
   D. I need a plier.

3. A. He bought the trouser at Macy's.
   B. He bought a trouser at Macy's.
   C. He bought the trousers at Macy's.
   D. He bought a trousers at Macy's.

4. A. She loves those new jeans.
   B. She loves that new jean.
   C. She loves a new jeans.
   D. She loves these new jean.

5. A. Is this pant for sale?
   B. Are this pants for sale?
   C. Is these pant for sale?
   D. Are these pants for sale?

6. A. His boxer was in the drawer.
   B. His boxers was in the drawer.
   C. His boxer were in the drawer.
   D. His boxers were in the drawer.

7. A. Her glass was in their case.
   B. Her glasses was in their case.
   C. Her glass were in their case.
   D. Her glasses were in their case.

8. A. You need this shear to cut that fabric.
   B. You need these shears to cut that fabric.
   C. You need these shear to cut those fabrics.
   D. You need this shears to cut that fabric.

9. A. Carrie cut her finger with a scissors.
   B. Carrie cut her finger with a scissor.
   C. Carrie cut her finger with the scissors.
   D. Carrie cut her finger with the scissor.

10. A. Carrie's glass were lost at school.
    B. Carrie's glasses were lost at school.
    C. Carrie's glasses at school were lost.
    D. Carrie's lost were glass at school.

✐ Irregular Plural Nouns

Singular	Plural –from Old English
man	men
woman	women
child	children
ox	oxen
mouse	mice
foot	feet
tooth	teeth

✐ Practice saying the irregular plural nouns.

Exercise 9.6

Multiple choice. Circle the letter in front of the correct sentence.

1. A. Thirty men run in the race.
   B. Thirty mans run in the race.
   C. Thirty men runs in the race.
   D. Thirty man runs in the race.

2. A. These womans wants to work.
   B. This women want to work.
   C. These women want to work.
   D. This women wants to work.

3. A. This mice likes cheese.
   B. This mouses like cheese.
   C. Those mouses likes cheese.
   D. Those mice like cheese.

4. A. They gave this childs milk.
   B. They gave those childs milk.
   C. They gave this children milk.
   D. They gave those children milk.

5. A. He brushed his tooths after he ate.
   B. He brushed his teeth after he ate.
   C. He brushed a teeth after he ate.
   D. He brushed the tooths after he ate.

6. A. She washed her feet in the shower.
   B. She washed a feet in the shower.
   C. She washed those foots in the shower.
   D. She washed her foots in the shower.

7. A. Farmers harnessed those oxs.
   B. Farmers harnessed those oxes.
   C. Farmers harnessed those ox.
   D. Farmers harnessed those oxen.

8. A. Childs love sweet food.
   B. Children love sweet food.
   C. Child love sweet food.
   D. Childes love sweet food.

9. A. Nine man are on the baseball team.
   B. Nine mans are on the baseball team.
   C. Nine mens are on the basebell team.
   D. Nine men are on the baseball team.

10. A. He heard his name and was on his feet.
    B. He heard his name and was on his foot.
    C. He heard his name and was on his foots.
    D. He heard his name and was on his feets.

11. A. Woman run the company.
    B. Womans run the company.
    C. Women run the company.
    D. Woman runs the company.

12. A. Man wrote those books.
    B. Men wrote those books.
    C. Mans wrote those books.
    D. Mens wrote those books.

13. A. Women wrote these books.
    B. Womans wrote these books.
    C. Woman wrote these books.
    D. Womens wrote these books.

14. A. He writes child's books.
    B. He writes childs's books.
    C. He writes childrens books.
    D. He writes children's books.

15. A. He has big foots.
    B. He has big foot.
    C. He has big feet.
    D. He has a big feet.

Exercise 9.7

Fill in. Write the correct word choice in each blank.

1. The __________ bought his __________ at J. C. Penney's.
   (man / men) (pant / pants)

2. __________ children run with __________.
   (Many / Much) (scissor / scissors)

3. The __________ like reading with their __________ up.
   (man / men) (feet / foot)

4. __________ children like __________.
   (Few / Little) (mice / mouse)

5. __________ have big __________.
   (Ox / Oxen) (feet / foot)

➾ Practice saying the sentences.

✐ Irregular Past Tense Verbs: Vowel Changes to E

Present tense	Past tense	Pronunciation
blow	blew	/ ū /
fall	fell	/ e /
fly	flew	/ ū /
grow	grew	/ ū /
hold	held	/ e /
know	knew	/ ū /
lead / lēd /	led	/ led /

➾ Practice saying the irregular past tense verbs.

Exercise 9.8

Multiple Choice. Circle the letter in front of the correct sentence.

1. A. She knowed the loyal faculty.
   B. She knewed the loyal faculty.
   C. She knew the loyal faculty.
   D. She known the loyal faculty.

2. A. The trees fell on the house.
   B. The trees falled on the house.
   C. The trees felled on the house.
   D. The tress fallen on the house.

3. A. The red roses grew.
   B. The red roses growed.
   C. The red roses grewed.
   D. The red roses grown.

4. A. He holded the child's pink hand.
   B. He hold the child's pink hand.
   C. He held the child's pink hand.
   D. He helded the child's pink hand.

5. A. They leaded the strong committee.
   B. They leads the strong committee.
   C. They led the strong committee.
   D. They lode the strong committee.

6. A. The wind blew out the orange fire.
   B. The wind blowed out the orange fire.
   C. The wind blow out the orange fire.
   D. The wind bloed out the orange fire.

7. A. Professors leaded class.
   B. Professors leads class.
   C. Professors led class.
   D. Professor leded class.

8. A. The children growed tall.
   B. The children grewed tall.
   C. The children grew tall.
   D. The children grown tall.

9. A. The airplane flied to Bangkok.
   B. The airplane flew to Bangkok.
   C. The airplane flewed to Bangkok
   D. The airplane flyed to Bangkok.

10. A. They knew the men.
   B. They knowed the men.
   C. They knewed the men.
   D. They known the men.

11. A. Kim helded two sharps knifes.
   B. Kim holded two sharps knives.
   C. Kim hold two sharp knifes.
   D. Kim held two sharp knives.

12. A. The orange leafs fell from the trees.
   B. The orange leaves falled from the trees.
   C. The orange leaves fell from the trees.
   D. The orange leaves felled from the trees.

13. A. Mike leaded the brown dog on a leash.
   B. Mike led the dog brown on a leash.
   C. Mike the brown dog led on a leash.
   D. Mike led the brown dog on a leash.

14. A. Dr. Jones complained about the pesticide toxic.
   B. Dr. Jones complained about the toxic pesticide.
   C. Dr. Jones about the toxic pesticide complained.
   D. Dr. Jones complend about the toxic pesticide.

15. A. Sally blowed out the last match.
   B. Sally blew out the last match.
   C. Sally out blew the last match.
   D. Sally the last match blew out.

Exercise 9.9

Fill in. Write the correct past tense verb in the blank.

1. Darryl ________ he passed the test.
   (know)

2. Mrs. Hernandez ______ the fish.
   (hold)

3. Sally ______ on her coffee.
   (blow)

4. Dave _______ about his application.
   (worry)

5. The ducks _____ across the park.
   (fly)

6. The storm _______ the trees down.
   (blow)

7. Tim ______ the project.
   (lead)

8. The redwood trees _____ on Dr. Carson's house.
   (fall)

9. Dr. Carson ________ Dr. An liked barbecued chicken.
   (know)

10. The motorcycle riders ______ the parade.
    (lead)

11. Henry ______ the cell phone.
    (hold)

12. Carrie ______ on the playground.
    (fall)

13. The dogs ______ with the ducks.
    (fight)

14. Dr. An ______ the cupcake.
    (hold)

15. John _____ his finger on the box.
(cut)

16. Shirley ______ clay for the craft store.
(buy)

17. Dr. An ______ class discussion.
(lead)

18 Dr. Jones ______ a meeting in the conference room.
(hold)

19. Emma ______ cupcakes to the restaurant.
(bring)

20. The students _______ the right answer for the quiz.
(know)

➾ Practice saying the sentences.

Speaking Activity: One partner asks the other the questions below inserting *many* or *much*. The other partner answers the questions in complete sentences using *many* or *much*. Then switch roles.

1. How _____________ rice did your family make?
2. How _____________ scoops of rice did you make?
3. How _____________ furniture do you have in your bedroom?
4. How _____________ chairs are there in your room?
5. How _____________ clothing do you pack for a weekend trip?
6. How _____________ pairs of socks do you pack for a weekend trip?
7. How _____________ students are in this class?
8. How _____________ books did you buy this semester?
9. How _____________ coffee / tea did you drink this morning?

10. How ____________ cups of coffee / tea did you drink last week?

11. How ____________ advice did you get about coming to this school?

Reading. Below is an e-mail from Emma Hernandez to her Korean pen pal Park Dae Sung. They have exchanged many letters. She is responding to questions he asked her in his last e-mail.

Hi Dae Sung,

Thank you so much for your letter telling me about your family and your school. I enjoyed learning about your life in South Korea. I wish I could go there, meet you, and see your home.

You asked about my room, what I do for fun, my mother's restaurant, and my father's luggage store.

My sister and I used to share a room, but I got my own room two years ago. I have a few posters of my favorite singers on the wall, such as Mariah Cary, Taylor Swift, and Pink. They are so pretty, and they wear such beautiful clothes. I wish I could be them, especially Pink. A few of my friends come over on the weekends, and we listen to many CDs and play a few video games in my room. My closet has many cute belts, purses, and pairs of shoes. I like the colors pink and black, so many of my things are pink or black. My walls and my computer are pink, and my TV and dresser are black. I wear my favorite skinny black jeans with my favorite black concert T-shirt and pink hightop tennis shoes. Sometimes my friends and I go to the mall on the weekends. I like to wear a little makeup when we go, and sometimes I put a little sparkle dust around my eyes just to stand out.

My favorite food at my mother's restaurant is the quiche. Quiche is a French dish with many eggs and much cream; it is very rich. It also has a little bacon and onion, so it has much flavor. My mother makes it every morning, and the lunch crowd loves it. Her restaurant is a five-minute walk from my school. I go there after school and do my homework. My mother gives me a ride home when she gets off work.

My father sells many briefcases, gym bags, and travel bags in his store. He also sells much luggage to business people and others who take long trips. Much of his stock is made of leather in the United States, Mexico, or China. A little of it is made in Bangladesh and Brazil. Many of his customers come to his store because he stocks leather items and items made in America.

Please tell me more about your room, what you do for fun, and your parents' work places. I hope to hear from you again soon.

Best wishes,
Emma

Comprehension activity.

1. What did Dae Sung tell Emma in his last letter?
2. What did Dae Sung ask Emma to tell him about?
3. What does Emma have on her walls?
4. What is in Emma's closet?
5. Which colors are Emma's favorites?
6. What kind of shoes does Emma like to wear?
7. Which ingredients make quiche so rich?
8. Where does Emma go after school every day?
9. What does Emma's father sell?
10. Where is his stock made?
11. What does Emma still want to know about Dae Sung?

Writing Activity: Write an e-mail to Emma. Respond to the questions she asks. Your e-mail begins "Hi Emma." Notice that the body of Emma's letter responds to Dae Sung's questions in the order he asks them. So, your letter to Emma should respond in the order of the questions she asks Dae Sung.

Chapter 10: Catching Up with Each Other

Grammar

Phrasal Verbs.

Dialogue

Dialogue for pronunciation and intonation. The teacher reads to the class, emphasizing pronunciation and intonation. The teacher reads Jesse's part while students read Mike's part. Students pair up and practice the dialogue, and then switch parts and practice again. The teacher corrects pronunciation and intonation.

Jesse	Hey, Mike, are you in there? Open up, it's Jesse.
Mike	Jesse! Man, I haven't seen you in awhile. Come in. Tell me why you're knocking on my door on a Saturday morning. I could have slept in for another hour.
Jesse	I'm sorry. I didn't call ahead because my tire blew out on the free-way just down the block.
Mike	Come in and sit down in the kitchen. I'll make some coffee. Do you need to call out?
Jesse	Thanks, no. The auto club already came out. They're trying to patch up my tire now.
Mike	I'm so glad to see you, man. It's been too many years, and I hope we can catch up with each other. Do you want some breakfast? I'm going to fry up some bacon and eggs.
Jesse	Do you still spice up the eggs with hot sauce?
Mike	Of course.
Jesse	Count me in.
Mike	Great. So, how are Liz and the girls?
Jesse	Liz is fine. The girls are fine. Liz still teaches high school French; she's a great teacher. Jessica took up the piano last year. She really loves it, and she's getting pretty good at it. Mary is getting good grades in English and loves to sing in the school chorus.
Mike	Oh, I'd love to see them again. We're going to have to make the time, my friend. Why don't I make dinner here and have you all over?

Jesse Sure. When were you thinking?

Mike Well, the semester just started, and I've got so much lesson planning to do for my literature classes. I'm also working on an essay. I think next month would be better.

Jesse I can do that. Let me check with Liz, though.

Mike How do you want your eggs?

Jesse Over easy.

Mike Then breakfast is ready.

Jesse Thank you. This looks tasty. You always knew your way around the kitchen. I heard about your dad. I'm so sorry, Mike.

Mike He passed away two months ago.

Jesse I know. I was in Germany on tour. I couldn't get away.

Mike I understand. It's alright. He had a full life. He got along with everyone and had many friends. My sister and I looked after him here in my house as soon as he got too sick to care for himself. He was pretty content.

Jesse Your father had a gentle spirit.

Mike He really did.

Jesse Do you remember when he taught us how to play *Maple Leaf Rag* on the piano?

Mike I remember I sounded awful and you sounded good. You were the musical son he never had.

Jesse I look back on that day every once in awhile. Do you know what I took away from that experience?

Mike Tell me.

Jesse If you take care of the little things, the big things take care of themselves.

Mike I picked up on that. It was a way my father had. He never fussed over the big things. He let people call him out, or even knock him down. Remember Hal at the hardware store that time? My dad just got up and went on his way. I was so embarrassed when Hal's son told me about it at school the next day.

Jesse He didn't hold onto anything bad. He let it all pass through him.

Mike He didn't. Nothing hurt him. When I was a kid, I thought he couldn't stand up for himself. But, what I took for weakness was actually a great strength. I didn't come up with that until he was living with me in my house, and I was taking care of him.

Jesse I realized it when we were eight years old learning to play *Maple Leaf Rag*. It was the way his fingers tapped the piano keys, and the way his voice just tapped at the air. He never used force.

Mike He let it all pass by.

Vocabulary

✓ Nouns and Indefinite Pronouns

anything
article
auto club
everything
experience
force
freeway
French
Germany
girl
hardware store
hot sauce
lesson planning
Maple Leaf Rag
month
nothing
piano
son
spirit
strength
teacher
things
tire
voice
weakness

✓ Adjectives

awful
big
content
fine
full
gentle
glad
good
great
little
musical
negative
over easy
quick
ready
sick
sorry
tasty

✓ Phrasal Verbs

blow out
call ____ out
call ahead
call out
catch up with
check with
come in
come out
come up with
count ___ in
fry up
fuss over
get along
get away
get up
go on ____ way
have _____ over
hear about
hold onto
knock down
knock on
look after
care for
look back

open up
pass away
pass by
pass through
patch up
pick up on
sit down
sleep in
spice up
stand up for
take away
know ___ way around
take care of
take up
tapped at

→ Practice saying the phrasal verbs.

Phrasal verbs are verbs followed by one or two prepositions, an adverb, or a preposition and an adverb. Phrasal verbs and their meanings need to be memorized.

Some phrasal verbs can be split up. Specifically, the preposition or adverb can come after the direct object.

- They *patched up* his tire. OK
- They *patched* his tire *up*. OK
- She *blew out* her birthday cake candles. OK
- She *blew* her birthday cake candles *out*. OK

The preposition in these phrasal verbs can come right after the verb or follow the object of the sentence. Practice saying the sentences.

Some phrasal verbs cannot be split up.

- I *called ahead* about visiting Mike's house. OK
- I *called* about visiting Mike's house *ahead*. NO
- Jesse *looked back* on his childhood years. OK
- Jesse *looked* on his childhood years *back*. NO

The preposition or adverb in these phrasal verbs must come right after the verb; it cannot follow the object. Practice saying the correct sentences.

✐ More Phrasal Verbs that Cannot be split up

break out
catch on
catch up with
check into
come across
come in
come out
come up with
end up with
get along with
get by
get over
get up
give in
go ahead
go back
grow up
keep up with
look after
look away
look down on
look up to
pass away
pick up on
put up with
run into
run out of
show up
sit down
stand up for

➾ Practice saying the phrasal verbs that cannot be split up.

Some phrasal verbs have to be split up when the object is a pronoun.

- This is going to *cheer* him *up*. OK
- This is going to *cheer up* him. NO
- We *figured* it *out*. OK
- We *figured out* it. NO
- You can *count* me *in*. OK
- You can *count in* me. NO
- They *called* him *out*. OK
- They *called out* him. NO
- We'll *be on* our *way*. OK
- We'll be *on way* our. NO
- She *knows* her *way around* a library. OK
- She *knows way around* her a library. NO
- We'll *have* you *over* for lunch tomorrow. OK
- We'll *have over* you for lunch tomorrow. NO

➾ Practice saying the correct sentences.

✅ More Phrasal Verbs that must be split up when a pronoun is the direct object

ask out
blow up
break in
break down
bring up
call back
cross out
do over
drop by
fill in
find out
give back
hand in
leave out
look over
make up
pass out
pick up
point out
put away
put on
show off
shut off
take back
take off
take out
tear down
tear up
think over
throw away
turn on
wear away
wear in
wear out

Exercise 10.1

Multiple choice. Circle the letter in front of the sentence with the correct word order and word choices.

1. A. They know around their way a restaurant.
   B. They know around the restaurant their way.
   C. They know their way around a restaurant.
   D. They know his way around a restaurant.

2. A. The paper she fills in.
   B. She the paper fills in.
   C. She fills in the paper.
   D. She in fills the paper.

3. A. I it never found out.
   B. I never found it out.
   C. It I never found out.
   D. I never found out it.

4. A. She left him out.
   B. She left out him.
   C. She him left out.
   D. Him she out left.

5. A. We picked the tasty hot sauce up.
   B. We picked hot sauce the tasty up.
   C. We picked up the tasty hot sauce.
   D. We hot sauce the picked up tasty.

6. A. He away threw his old piano.
   B. He threw his away old piano.
   C. He his old piano threw away.
   D. He threw his old piano away.

7. A. She in Los Angeles gets by on her own.
   B. She gets on her own by in Los Angeles.
   C. She gets in Los Angeles by on her own.
   D. She gets by in Los Angeles on her own.

8. A. The thieves broke to Hal's hardware store in.
   B. The thieves broke in to Hal's hardware store.
   C. The thieves broke Hal's hardware store in to.
   D. The thieves Hal's hardware store broke in to.

9. A. I will check into it.
   B. I will check it into.
   C. I will it check into.
   D. I will into check it.

10. A. I came across your book yesterday.
    B. I came your book across yesterday.
    C. I came your book yesterday across.
    D. I your book came across yesterday.

11. A. He kept up with his homework.
    B. He kept with his homework up.
    C. He kept with up his homework.
    D. He his homework kept up with.

12. A. They ran of soap out in the bathroom.
    B. They ran soap out of in the bathroom.
    C. They ran out of soap the bathroom in.
    D. They ran out of soap in the bathroom.

13. A. She is getting over her cold.
    B. She is getting her cold over.
    C. She is getting cold her over.
    D. She her cold is getting over.

14. A. They got late up yesterday.
    B. They got late yesterday up.
    C. They got up late yesterday.
    D. They late got up yesterday.

15. A. Emma grew in California up.
    B. Emma grew up in California.
    C. Emma grew California in up.
    D. Emma in California grew up.

16. A. I won't go with you back.
    B. I won't go back with you.
    C. I with you won't go back.
    D. I you won't with back go.

17. A. I ran Jesse into yesterday.
    B. I ran into Jesse yesterday.
    C. I into Jesse ran yesterday.
    D. I yesterday ran into Jesse.

18. A. My professor it looked over last week.
    B. My professor looked it over last week.
    C. My professor looked over it last week.
    D. My professor looked last week over it.

19. A. I handed in homework my on time.
    B. I handed in on time my homework.
    C. I my homework handed in on time.
    D. I handed my homework in on time.

20. A. Can I make up last week's quiz?
    B. Can I last week's quiz make up?
    C. Can I make last up week's quiz?
    D. Can I quiz make up last week's?

21. A. Did you the papers give back yet?
    B. Did you give the papers yet back?
    C. Did you give the papers back yet?
    D. Did you the papers yet give back?

22. A. Could I drop your office by during office hours?
    B. Could I during office hours drop by your office?
    C. Could I drop by your office during office hours?
    D. Could drop by your office I during office hours?

23. A. The professor the syllabus passed out last week.
    B. The professor passed out last week the syllabus.
    C. The professor passed the syllabus out last week.
    D. The professor passed the out syllabus last week.

24. A. Could I my paper do over?
    B. Could I do my over paper?
    C. Could I do my paper over?
    D. Could do my I over paper?

25. A. I cannot put up with noisy children.
    B. I cannot with noisy children put up.
    C. I cannot noisy with children put up.
    D. I cannot put noisy children with up.

Exercise 10.2

Sentence Building. Put the following statements and questions in the correct word order. Statements begin with a capital letter and end with a period. Questions begin with a capital letter and end with a question mark.

1. Jesse / Mike's father / caught on / to

   ____

2. I / sweater / old / my / came across / closet / my / in

   ____

3. I / to sit down / want / a minute / for

   ____

4. daughter / my / me / looks up to

   ____

5. you / did / friend / your / run into / party / at the / ?

   ____

6. he / cold / his / got over

____

7. student / shy / the / professor / the / from / looks away

____

8. seniors / freshmen / look down on

____

9. professor / the / chalk / ran out of

____

10. you / did / score / bad / a / how / end up with / ?

____

11. I / class / the / keep up with

____

12. students / good / do not / students / lazy / put up with

____

13. student / the / class / late for / showed up

____

14. you / would / come in / ?

____

15. we / lesson / to the / could / go back / ?

____

16. Dr. Carson / this / class / to the / pointed out

____

17. Kim / essay / her / in class / handed in

____

18. Henry / application / his / yesterday / filled in

____

19. you / did / how / to this business / break in / ?

____

20. Darryl / paper / his / wants / to do over

____

21. he / quiz he missed / the / to make up / asked

____

22. you / would / homework / my / look over / ?

____

23. Darryl / Kim / to ask out / wants

____

24. Carrie / house / Susan's / on weekends / drops by

____

25. you / how can / this / throw away / ?

____

26. student / the / wrong answer / the / crossed out

____

27. you / did / TV / the / turn on / ?

____

28. you / have / problem / the / figured out / ?

____

29. I / why he / found out / ran away

____

30. you / could / quizzes / the / pass out / ?

____

➾ Practice saying the sentences.

Speaking Activity 1: Partners take turns asking and answering the following questions using the phrasal verbs given below. Say the phrasal verbs in the questions and in the answers.

Phrasal Verbs that Cannot Be Split up

- How did you catch up with your homework?
- Where did you come across your class notes?
- When did she come in to the classroom?
- When did you come out of the classroom?
- What answer did you come up with?
- How did he end up with an A?
- Do you get along with your classmates?
- How did the teacher get back to the lesson plan?
- How did the teacher go ahead to the next lesson?
- What do you do when your pen runs out of ink?
- How did the teacher get the students to show up on time?
- How did the teacher get the students to sit down for the lesson?

Speaking Activity 2: Partners take turns asking and answering the following questions using the phrasal verbs given below. Say the phrasal verbs in the questions and in the answers. When you answer the questions below, insert a pronoun between the verb and the preposition.

Phrasal Verbs that must be split up when a pronoun is the direct object

- Can you break down the problem for me?
- Would you like to bring up a question?
- Did you check out this week's assignment?
- Can you cheer up your friend?
- Why did you cross out your answer?
- May I do the homework over?
- How did you figure out the answer?
- Who filled in the blanks?
- When will the teacher give back the homework?
- When will the students hand in the homework?
- How can I make up the quiz?
- When did you pass out the syllabus?
- Where can I pick up my paper?
- Would you put away your books?
- Did you shut off the lights?
- Would you turn on the lights?

✓ Irregular Past Tense Verbs: Vowel Changes to O

Present tense	Pro.	Past tense	Pro.
break	/ ā /	broke	/ ō /
choose	/ ū /	chose	/ ō /
drive	/ ī /	drove	/ ō /
get	/ e /	got	/ o /
ride	/ ī /	rode	/ ō /
speak	/ ē /	spoke	/ ō /
tear	/ e /	tore	/ ō /
wear	/ e /	wore	/ ō /
write	/ ī /	wrote	/ ō /

Exercise 10.3

Multiple choice. Circle the letter in front of the sentence with the correct past tense verb or phrasal verb form.

1. A. He writed a letter to a friend.
   B. He write a letter to a friend.
   C. He wrote a letter to a friend.
   D. He writted a letter to a friend.

2. A. We speaked up to the teacher.
   B. We spoke up to the teacher.
   C. We spoken up to the teacher.
   D. We spoke to the teacher up.

3. A. He getted up in the morning.
   B. He gotted up in the morning.
   C. He got up in the morning.
   D. He getten up in the morning.

4. A. You wore in your new shoes.
   B. You weared in your new shoes.
   C. You wear your in new shoes.
   D. You wored in your new shoes.

5. A. They breaked out of jail.
   B. They broke out of jail.
   C. They broked out of jail.
   D. They broke of jail out.

6. A. We chose pot roast for dinner.
   B. We choosed pot roast for dinner.
   C. We chosed pot roast for dinner.
   D. We chosen pot roast for dinner.

7. A. We rode a horse.
   B. We rided a horse.
   C. We ridden a horse.
   D. We roded a horse.

8. A. I spoked out against the war.
   B. I speaked out against the war.
   C. I spoke out against the war.
   D. I spoke against the war out.

9. A. They weared out their uniforms.
   B. They wore out their uniforms.
   C. They wored out their uniforms.
   D. They wear their uniforms out.

10. A. He broke down and cried.
    B. He breaked down and cried.
    C. He broken down and cried.
    D. He broke down and cryed.

11. A. They gotted back to the house.
    B. They got back to the house.
    C. They getted back to the house.
    D. They got to the house back.

12. A. We drove to the highway.
    B. We drived to the highway.
    C. We droved to the highway.
    D. We driven to the highway.

13. A. Emma speaked up in class.
    B. Emma spoke in class up.
    C. Emma spoke up in class.
    D. Emma spoked up in class.

14. A. Henry and Susan writted a letter to their uncle.
    B. Henry and Susan wrote a letter to their uncle.
    C. Henry and Susan write a letter to their uncle.
    D. Henry and Susan wroted a letter to their uncle.

15. A. I chose to go to college.
    B. I chosed to go to college.
    C. I choosed to go to college.
    D. I chosen to go to college.

16. A. Tim get down to business.
    B. Tim getted down to business.
    C. Tim got down to business.
    D. Tim got to business down.

17. A. Kim broke her cell phone.
    B. Kim breaked her cell phone.
    C. Kim broked her cell phone.
    D. Kim broken her cell phone.

18. A. The professor speak out to the administration.
    B. The professor spoke out to the administration.
    C. The professor spoke to the administration out.
    D. The professor spoked out to the administration.

19. A. Kim and Tim rided the bus to work.
    B. Kim and Tim ridden the bus to work.
    C. Kim and Tim rode the bus to work.
    D. Kim and Tim roded the bus to work.

20. A. Todd broke the pot.
    B. Todd breaked the pot.
    C. Todd broked the pot.
    D. Todd broken the pot.

21. A. The pyraminds wore in the wind away.
    B. The pyramids wore away in the wind.
    C. The pyramids weared away in the wind.
    D. The pyramids wear away in the wind.

22. A. The dog teared up my shoes.
    B. The dog tear up my shoes.
    C. The dog tore up my shoes.
    D. The dog tore my up shoes.

23. A. The city tore the old down house.
    B. The city teared down the old house.
    C. The city tear down the old house.
    D. The city tore the old house down.

24. A. Carrie tore her homework up.
    B. Carrie tear up her homework.
    C. Carrie teared up her homework.
    D. Carrie tore her up homework.

25. A. Mike breaked the wall down.
    B. Mike break the wall down.
    C. Mike breaked down wall the.
    D. Mike broke the wall down.

Exercise 10.4

Fill in the blanks turning the verb below into the past tense and adding any necessary preposition(s) and / or adverb to form the phrasal verb.

1. The thief _______ to the house.
   (break)

2. Dr. Carson ______ the syllabus.
   (pass)

3. Dr. An _____ the homework before sending us home to work on it.
   (go)

4. Kim ______ her research paper to Dr. Carson.
   (hand)

5. Jill _______ the quiz she missed last week.
   (make)

6. Andrea _______ a very interesting question.
   (bring)

7. Dr. Jones ______ chalk during class.
   (run)

8. Kim ______ for class on time.
   (show)

9. Darryl _______ the problem into five parts.
   (break)

10. Dr. An ______ the graded tests.
(give)

11. Henry bought a new pair of boots when he ______ the old ones.
(wear)

12. I was so angry I _____ your letter.
(tear)

13. Carrie ______ the wrong answer on her test.
(cross)

14. Emma's letters _______ Dae Sung.
(cheer)

15. The students _____ at their desks.
(sit)

16. Susan _____ with everyone because she was so nice.
(get)

17. Darryl _____ with an A in African American literature.
(end)

18. Dr. An _______ my paper yesterday and advised me to change my topic.
(look)

19. They _______ the lights in the classroom.
(turn)

20. The H1N1 virus _______ last year.
(break)

➾ Practice saying the sentences.

Reading. This is an e-mail from Jill to Henry. She is asking questions about a class they have together at the university.

Dear Henry,

Hi, it's Jill. I have some questions for you. I didn't run into you today at Starbucks, so I'm writing. I missed our Asian literature class on Thursday. Could I look over your class notes? I want to be caught up before I ask Dr. An any follow-up questions during her office hours on Tuesday.

Additionally, I liked the point you brought up in class last week about the theme of the wilderness in literature. I wrote a paper on that topic in Dr. Carson's class last semester, so I'd like to get into that with you sometime. I'm starting a study group. Let me know if you want to get together with us, and I'll get back to you about times to meet. Right now it's just me and Kim Tapscott. I know you two get along with each other. We get together some Monday nights in the study area on the third floor of the library.

I also want to thank you for telling me and Andrea about your mother's restaurant. We dropped by the other day and checked it out. I looked over the whole menu. Andrea came across the empanadas, and that was all she wanted. I had to think it over a while. Then your mother talked up the quiche, so I had to have it. Her food is really great.

Have a nice weekend!

Regards,
Jill

Comprehension activity.

1. Why is Jill writing to Henry?
2. Which class do Jill and Henry have together?
3. Who is Jill going to talk to after she looks at Henry's notes?
4. Which topic are Jill and Henry both interested in?
5. What kind of group is Jill starting?
6. What will Henry need to know to meet with Jill and Kim?

7. How did Jill find out about Mrs. Hernandez's restaurant?

8. How did Andrea find out about the empanadas?

9. How did Jill find out about the quiche?

10. What did Jill think of Mrs. Hernandez's food?

Writing Activity: Write an e-mail to a classmate whom you know pretty well. In your e-mail, tell your peer who you are and why you are writing. Ask a couple of questions about class topics or getting together to study. In addition, suggest an activity to do together, such as having a meal at a restaurant, going shopping, or seeing a play or a movie. Use at least ten phrasal verbs in your e-mail.

Chapter 11: Enjoying the Outdoors

Grammar

Adverbs, Negative Adverbs, Conjunctive Adverbs, and Their Placement.

Dialogue

Dialogue for pronunciation and intonation. The teacher reads to the class, emphasizing pronunciation and intonation. The teacher reads Sarah's part while students read Tim's part. Students pair up and practice the dialogue, and then switch parts and practice again. The teacher corrects pronunciation and intonation.

Sarah	Tim, hi. How are you?
Tim	Hello, Sarah. I'm doing fine. How are you?
Sarah	Good, good. Your group is moving quickly on the koi pond.
Tim	Yes, it goes well. We want to finish digging the hole tonight, and then start covering it tomorrow.
Sarah	It is good you gave yourselves enough time to cover the bottom completely.
Tim	We're following your instructions closely.
Sarah	Your work is going beautifully.
Tim	We are all enjoying the chance to work outdoors in the sun. It's spring. It's a beautiful day. The sun is shining, the birds are chirping.
Sarah	Yes, it's very nice outside. I am so grateful for the California weather. However, I need to talk to you seriously about the aquatic plants for the pond.
Tim	OK, great. I have been anxiously awaiting this part of the project.
Sarah	Don Wing can get the cattails for us soon. However, I asked him to hold off until next week when we're ready.
Tim	OK. So, what's the problem?
Sarah	Well, it is unlikely we can get the lotus plants here in the valley. We may have to put those off indefinitely.

Tim	Are there other varieties of lotus to consider? For example, we can choose varieties that do not bloom regularly, or that never bloom locally.
Sarah	The local nurseries rarely carry those. However, the university nursery might actually consider growing lotus for the pond. Still, that usually takes time.
Tim	I understand. The koi fish come in next week too, right?
Sarah	Koi fish are easily come by in central California. Many local breeders always have koi in a variety of colors. There are usually koi shows in the spring and summer months. I just told Carl about one coming up in Fig Blossom Fair. He seemed excited to go.
Tim	He'll choose well. Carl has never been without fish. Also, he knows well how to look after them.
Sarah	In addition, this brings up my next point. Deborah is not so sure we should use the plastic we so thoughtfully chose in the beginning. She thinks we really need a thicker barrier between the soil and the water because the soil is more acidic than we thought before. As a result, the acid could badly hurt the fish.
Tim	How much more will this cost?
Sarah	About fifty dollars.
Tim	OK. I think we can easily afford it, but I should get back to the books now and check out our budget.
Sarah	Yes, I'm pretty sure you're right. Finally, before you go, I need you to do a bit of work for me.
Tim	OK.
Sarah	Please check out the grass on the campus south lawn. Look at it closely. I think it really needs more water.
Tim	Of course. I will. See you tomorrow.
Sarah	Good work, Tim. Have a good night.

Vocabulary

✓ Adverbs

actually
always
anxiously
badly
beautifully
completely
closely
easily
fine
indefinitely

later
locally
now
quickly
rarely
really
recently
regularly
seriously
so
soon
thoughtfully
too
unlikely
usually
very
well

Adverbs describe verbs, adjectives, other adverbs, prepositional phrases, clauses, and sentences. Adverbs describe how something happens (for example, *quickly* or *slowly*), in what way it happens (for example, *easily* or *badly*), when (*soon*; *never*) or where (*nationally*; *locally*), or to what degree (*completely*; *partially*) something happens. Most adverbs end in "ly," but some do not.

✐ Negative Adverbs

never
not

Negative adverbs come after modal verbs: for example, She *does not* go to school; He *did not* like the man; We *could not* drive the car; and, I *cannot* live like this. (Note that "cannot" is one word.) Nevertheless, negative adverbs come before other verbs: for example, She *never went* to school; He did *not like* the man; We *never drove* the car; and, We *cannot live* like this.

✐ Conjunctive Adverbs

also
as a result
finally
for example
however
in addition
of course
still
then

Conjunctive adverbs come at the beginning of a statement, and they show how that statement is related to the statement before it. In this way, they describe independent clauses. Identify the conjunctive adverbs in the dialogue.

✓ Verbs

afford
await
be without
bloom
come by
consider
cover
dig
enjoy
finish
follow
hold off
move
put off
shine

✓ Nouns

acid
aquatic plants
barrier
bottom
breeder
budget
cattail
chance
koi show
hole
instruction
lotus
nursery
part
plastic
point
project
soil
south
summer
the books
variety

✓ Adjectives

acidic
excited
local
thicker

Adverb Placement and the Object of the Verb

Adverbs can go in three different places in a sentence when the object of the verb is an indirect object:

- He works *quickly* on the koi pond. OK
- He works on the koi pond *quickly*. OK
- He *quickly* works on the koi pond. OK

All three sentences above are acceptable. The adverb can follow the verb, follow the indirect object of the verb, or come between the subject and the verb.

However, when the verb takes a direct object, the adverb cannot come between the verb and the direct object:

- He kicked the ball *quickly.* OK
- He *quickly* kicked the ball. OK
- He kicked *quickly* the ball. NO

Adverbs describe verbs, adjectives, other adverbs, and even whole clauses. However, adverbs do not describe nouns and pronouns: only adjectives describe nouns and pronouns. Adverbs are used to answer such questions as *how, how much, how often, where,* and *when.*

Exercise 11.1

Circle the letter in front of the sentence with the correct word order.

1. A. Tim not did put off the project.
   B. Tim did put off not the project.
   C. Tim did not put off the project.
   D. Tim did put off the not project.

2. A. They slowly to the store walked.
   B. They to the store walked slowly.
   C. Slowly they walked to the store.
   D. They walked slowly to the store.

3. A. You play the piano beautifully.
   B. You play beautifully the piano.
   C. You play the beautifully piano.
   D. You the piano play beautifully.

4. A. He waited anxiously for the professor.
   B. He waited for anxiously the professor.
   C. He waited for the anxiously professor.
   D. He anxiously for waited the professor.

5. A. Kim listened to the closely lecture.
   B. Kim listened to closely the lecture.
   C. Listened closely Kim to the lecture.
   D. Kim listened closely to the lecture.

6. A. The quickly flowers bloomed.
   B. The flowers bloomed quickly.
   C. Bloomed the flowers quickly.
   D. Quickly the flowers bloomed.

7. A. Tim thoughtfully waited for his sister.
   B. Tim waited for his thoughtfully sister.
   C. Tim waited thoughtfully his sister for.
   D. Tim his sister waited thoughtfully for.

8. A. I then strongly suggest you follow my instruction.
   B. Then, I strongly suggest you follow my instruction.
   C. I then suggest you strongly follow for my instruction.
   D. Then, I suggest you follow my strongly instruction.

9. A. The sun shone never on that part of the yard.
   B. Never the sun shone on that part of the yard.
   C. The sun shone on that never part of the yard.
   D. The sun never shone on that part of the yard.

10. A. I considered of course your idea.
    B. I considered your of course idea.
    C. Of course, I considered your idea.
    D. Of course, I your idea considered.

11. A. Locally I can buy cattails.
    B. I can buy cattails locally.
    C. I can buy locally cattails.
    D. I locally buy cattails can.

12. A. She rarely considers buying local food.
    B. She considers buying rarely local food.
    C. She considers buying local rarely food.
    D. Rarely she considers buying local food.

13. A. I cover my mouth still when I cough.
    B. I cover my still mouth when I cough.
    C. Still, I cover my mouth when I cough.
    D. I cover my mouth when I still cough.

14. A. I take usually chances.
    B. I usually take chances.
    C. I usually chances take.
    D. Take I usually chances.

15. A. Stella finishes my regularly sentences.
    B. Regularly Stella finishes my sentences.
    C. Stella regularly finishes my sentences.
    D. Stella my sentences regularly finishes.

16. A. This nicely plant goes in my yard.
    B. This plant goes in my nicely yard.
    C. This plant goes in yard my nicely.
    D. This plant goes nicely in my yard.

17. A. He go cannot without food indefinitely.
    B. Indefinitely cannot he go without food.
    C. He cannot go without food indefinitely.
    D. He without food cannot indefinitely go.

18. A. We do without fine instructions.
    B. We do fine without instructions.
    C. We fine do without instructions.
    D. Fine we do without instructions.

19. A. She kissed him warmly on the cheek.
    B. She kissed warmly him on the cheek.
    C. She kissed him on the warmly cheek.
    D. She kissed him on warmly the cheek.

20. A. Emma greets her warmly uncle and aunt.
    B. Emma greets her uncle and warmly aunt.
    C. Emma her uncle and aunt warmly greets.
    D. Emma warmly greets her uncle and aunt.

21. A. Mike's father plays the softly piano.
    B. Mike's father plays the piano softly.
    C. Mike's softly father plays the piano.
    D. Mike's father plays softly the piano.

22. A. Darryl plays the sweetly saxophone.
    B. Darryl plays sweetly the saxophone.
    C. Darryl plays the saxophone sweetly.
    D. Sweetly plays Darryl the saxophone.

23. A. In addition, I like the French horn.
    B. I like in addition the French horn.
    C. I like the French horn in addition.
    D. I in addition like the French horn.

24. A. This summer for example is hotter than last summer.
    B. This summer is for example hotter than last summer.
    C. This summer is hotter for example than last summer.
    D. For example, this summer is hotter than last summer.

25. A. Finally, he loved fish.
    B. He loved finally fish.
    C. He loved fish finally.
    D. He fish finally loved.

Exercise 11.2

Put the following sentences in a correct word order. There may be more than one correct way to complete some of the sentences.

1. she / instructions / rarely / followed

   ____

2. sun / the / December / in / shine / doesn't

   ____

3. this / flower / lotus / a / nice / for example / is

   ____

4. she / him / put off / of course

   ____

5. Sarah / trees / maple / the / locally grown / enjoyed

   ____

6. incense / the / room / the / scented / sweetly

   ____

7. project / this / half over / is / in addition

   ____

8. Mike / call / doctor's / the / patiently / awaited

   ____

9. I / no / cannot / indefinitely / say

____

10. he / chances / his / likes / also

____

11. point / their / true / is / likely

____

12. Henry / car / new / a / badly / wants

____

13. it / day / nice / a / is / still

____

14. Sarah / books / the / regularly / checked

____

15. I / hole / that / want / never / to dig

____

➾ Practice saying the sentences.

👤 Speaking Activity: Partners make up a dialogue about your day using all of the adverbs, conjunctive adverbs, negative adverbs, and verb phrases below.

What do you do first when you get up in the morning?

✓ Conjunctive Adverbs

First	Third
Second	Finally

✓ Adverbs

quickly	always
slowly	usually
cheerfully	sometimes
grumpily	once in a while

✓ Verb Phrases

get up	get dressed
eat breakfast	brush my hair
take a shower	walk to campus
comb my hair	drive to campus
brush my teeth	go to class

What don't you do when you come home in the evening?

➾ Negative Adverbs

do not	rarely
never	

➾ Verb Phrases

study	play video games
watch TV	wash clothes
listen to music	wash dishes

Reading. Below is an e-mail from Joong inviting his cousin Dave to join him and his new wife Stella on a skiing trip.

Dear Dave,

Hi, cousin. What's up? Stella and I are up in the mountains for the weekend. Much snow fell recently, so we came to ski. I know you always hike in the mountains in the summer. However, I strongly suggest you try cross-country skiing in the winter. Stella is a very good skier, and I learned quickly by closely following her instruction. When you ski cross-country, you move slowly across the flats. It's not as risky as downhill skiing. It's more like rollerblading, but with better scenery.

We would seriously like you to come up here with us next weekend. You do not want to miss this. We could leave immediately after we eat breakfast on Saturday morning. It's so beautiful up here. The snow falls softly on the pine trees and stretches out ubiquitously down the slopes like a great white blanket. The tall pines, cedars, and redwoods are all we see regularly on the forest floor. We rarely hear a sound, except the crunching of powder under our skiis. In addition, the exercise is greatly improving my leg strength. It would not hurt you to try it.

Also, you and I rarely have the chance to get out in the woods together since we finished college. It's really nice to come up here with Stella; however, having another guy on the trip would suit me nicely. Also, Stella's friend Andrea is coming, and we think the two of you would get along well. Andrea is a performing arts major at the university. She's really fun and smart, and devastatingly pretty. You will seriously lose your mind over her.

Finally, I hope you have the day off from the store. Let me know if you're interested.

Take care, man,
Joong

Comprehension activity.

1. Where is Joong?
2. When did the snow fall?
3. What does Dave usually do in the mountains?
4. What does Joong want Dave to do?
5. What did Stella teach Joong?
6. What is cross-country skiing like?
7. When does Joong want Dave to leave with him?
8. What does Joong say the snow does?
9. What do Joong and Stella see and hear in the forest?
10. Why does Joong want Dave to meet Andrea?

Writing Activity: Write an e-mail inviting a friend or relative to join you for an activity. Include a different adverb in each sentence of the letter.

Chapter 12: Talking About College Majors

Grammar

Participles, Gerunds, and Infinitives.

Dialogue

Dialogue for pronunciation and intonation. The teacher reads to the class, emphasizing pronunciation and intonation. The teacher reads Henry's part while students read Darryl's part. Students pair up and practice the dialogue, and then switch parts and practice again. The teacher corrects pronunciation and intonation.

Darryl Hey, Henry, wait up!
Henry Darryl, hi. What's going on?
Darryl The group is getting together this Friday at George's downtown. Do you want to sit in with us?
Henry You got it, Darryl. Playing drums with you guys is always fun. What time were you thinking about?
Darryl We have to be there at nine-thirty sharp.
Henry Is Terry going to be there?
Darryl She's going to play the bass for us.
Henry That is excellent. Have you decided on a set list yet?
Darryl I have an idea. Why? Do you want to add something?
Henry I wrote a song, and I want to play it with you and Terry.
Darryl Nice! What does it sound like? Can we learn it quickly?
Henry How about coming by my place tonight around seven o'clock?
Darryl Yes, I can make that.
Henry Come over, and I can play it for you.
Darryl Fine, fine. Hey, didn't you have Dr. Carson last semester?
Henry African American literature, yes I had his class. Are you enjoying it?
Darryl Reading the poetry and short stories is an eye-opening experience. This is definitely my best semester in college. I have never learned so much and enjoyed it so much before.
Henry You mean in an English class?
Darryl Definitely in an English class, but I'm thinking about changing my major.

Henry He's that good?
Darryl Definitely.
Henry Before you go changing your major, you should get to know more about what can be done with a degree in English. Do you want to be a teacher?
Darryl Well, maybe. But I could also be getting ready for law school or a career in publishing or politics.
Henry Really?
Darryl Really. English majors can go into advertising, marketing, or public relations. Also, teaching isn't such a bad job.
Henry I take it you have never tutored English.
Darryl No. What do you know about tutoring?
Henry I am a tutor in the English Department Writing Center.
Darryl You are kidding. How did you get that job?
Henry I applied for it, and I got an interview. I was hired this semester.
Darryl Do you want to be an English teacher?
Henry I did. Well, I think I still do. But it is really hard figuring out how to explain why somebody's writing doesn't make sense.
Darryl What do you mean "explain"? Don't you just rewrite the paper for them?
Henry What? No. You have to show students what they did wrong. You have to explain it so that they can correct their own mistakes. Otherwise, they just keep making the same mistakes and never improving.
Darryl So, what kinds of mistakes do they make?
Henry Many students need help coming up with ideas for their papers.
Darryl Isn't it cheating to give them your ideas?
Henry I don't give them my ideas. I help them by asking them questions.
Darryl So, are you becoming an expert in asking questions?
Henry Yeah. I know it sounds funny, but I am not wasting my time. It is actually helping me write my own papers.
Darryl So, the students are helping you?
Henry No, asking the questions is helping me. Also, I think reading their revisions is helping me.
Darryl How does that work?
Henry It is hard to explain. Somehow, watching other people go through the process of coming up with ideas and making an outline for those ideas helps me to have better arguments and better reasoning to support those arguments. Somehow, going through other students' papers from the first draft to the last helps me to write better drafts for my own classes and to have an easier time revising them.

Darryl OK. I guess all that work with other people gives you many opportunities to think about how an essay goes together, and to think about which ways of putting your thoughts together on paper are more successful than others.

Henry Yes, that's it!

Darryl Is the Writing Center hiring for next semester? I think I want to apply.

Henry I can get you the information tonight. Right now, I have to go to the Writing Center.

Darryl Good enough. See you later. Thanks!

Henry See you tonight.

Vocabulary

✓ Participles

becoming	getting
changing	going
coming	helping
coming up with	hired
decided	hiring
done*	improving
enjoyed	learned
enjoying	making
eye-opening	thinking
figuring	wasting
getting	

Participles have the base form of verbs and an ending. Present tense participles end in *ing*. Regular past tense participles end in *ed*. **Done* is an irregular past participle. Participles are used with linking verbs to form different verb tenses, and by themselves as adjectives.

✓ Gerunds

advertising	going
asking	making
cheating	marketing
coming up with	playing

publishing
reading
reasoning
revising
teaching
tutoring
watching
writing

Gerunds are nouns formed the same way as participles.

✐ Infinitives

to add
to apply
to be
to explain
to give
to go
to have
to know
to play
to show
to sit in
to support
to think
to write

Infinitives begin with the word *to* and end with the base form of a verb. They are not verbs. They may be nouns, adjectives, or adverbs.

Note that when *to* comes before a verb, it forms an infinitive phrase. When *to* comes before a noun, it forms a prepositional phrase.

✐ Other Nouns

argument
bass
draft
drum
expert
interview
law school
literature
mistake
opportunity
outline
poetry
politics
process
public relations
revision
sense
set list
short stories
thought
writing center

✐ Verbs

apply
come over
go into
learn
rewrite
sound
wait up

Linking verbs link the subject of a sentence to a noun or adjective (which is sometimes a participle, gerund, or infinitive) that comes after the verb.

✐ Linking Verbs: Forms of the Verb be

am	is
are	was
be	were
been	will be (future tense)
being	

✐ Linking Verbs: Sensory Verbs (sight, smell, etc.)

appears	smells
feels	sounds
looks	tastes
seems	

Every sentence requires a verb. Participles, gerunds, and infinitives are not verbs. Below are sentences with linking verbs. Some of them include a participle, infinitive, or gerund.

- We *are learning* English.
- She *is being* difficult.
- She *seems to like* the cold.
- This shirt *feels soft.*
- This flower *smells* sweet.
- He *appears* to be angry.

The items above are sentences because they all have a subject and a verb. The items below are not sentences because they do not have verbs.

- We learning English.
- She being difficult.
- It to be cold in here.
- He to be angry.

Exercise 12.1

Circle the letter in front of the complete, correct, and meaningful sentences.

1. A. He to change his college major.
   B. He wants to change his college major.
   C. He change his college major.
   D. He changes to want his college major.

2. A. We is thinking about studying poetry.
   B. We thinking about were studying poetry.
   C. We were thinking about studying poetry.
   D. We were think about study poetry.

3. A. Cheat is not permitted in college.
   B. Cheating not permitted in college.
   C. Cheats is not permitted in college.
   D. Cheating is not permitted in college.

4. A. Darryl is explaining it to her.
   B. Darryl explaining it to her.
   C. Darryl is explain it to her.
   D. Darryl be explaining it to her.

5. A. He is going to graduate in the fall.
   B. He going to graduate in the fall.
   C. He is go to graduate in the fall.
   D. He is goes to graduate in the fall.

6. A. They are ask if you will go.
   B. They be asking if you will go.
   C. They are asking if you will go.
   D. They are asks if you will goes.

7. A. Mike wanted watch TV.
   B. Mike wanted to watching TV.
   C. Mike to watch TV.
   D. Mike wanted to watch TV.

8. A. Is he go to come up with the answer soon?
   B. Are he going to come up with the answer soon?
   C. Is he to go to come up with the answer soon?
   D. Is he going to come up with the answer soon?

9. A. Have you been tutoring long?
   B. Have you tutoring long?
   C. Have you been tutor long?
   D. Have you been to tutor long?

10. A. Samsung is advertise new cell phone on TV.
    B. Samsung is advertising new cell phones on TV.
    C. Samsung advertising new cell phone on TV.
    D. Samsung to advertising new cell phone on TV.

11. A. This company will be publishing my book.
    B. This company will publishing my book.
    C. This company to publish my book.
    D. This company to be publishing my book.

12. A. Terry will sitting in with the band.
    B. Terry will be sitting in with the band.
    C. Terry will be sit in with the band.
    D. Terry will to sit in with the band.

13. A. He is go to decide tomorrow.
    B. He is going to decide tomorrow.
    C. He going to decide tomorrow.
    D. He is to go to decide tomorrow.

14. A. She was to hiring yesterday.
    B. She be hired yesterday.
    C. She was hired yesterday.
    D. She were hired yesterday.

15. A. Toyota's to market division will have a job to do.
    B. Toyota's marketing division will have a job to do.
    C. Toyota's marketing division will have a job to doing.
    D. Toyota's marketing division will a job to do.

16. A. Carrie going to play with Susan today.
    B. Carrie is go to play with Susan today.
    C. Carrie is going to playing with Susan today.
    D. Carrie is going to play with Susan today.

17. A. Susan is coming over to Carrie's house later.
    B. Susan coming over to Carrie's house later.
    C. Susan be coming over to Carrie's house later.
    D. Susan is to coming over to Carrie's house later.

18. A. He going to come up with the answer in a minute.
    B. He is go to come up with the answer in a minute.
    C. He is going to come up with the answer in a minute.
    D. He is going coming up with the answer in a minute.

19. A. They appearing to give their attention to the professor.
    B. They appear to give their attention to the professor.
    C. They appear to giving their attention to the professor.
    D. They appearing giving their attention to the professor.

20. A. This steak appears being cooked.
    B. This steak appearing being cooked.
    C. This steak appears to be cooked.
    D. This steak to appear to be cooked.

21. A. To reason is the most important skill taught.
    B. Reasoning be the most important skill taught.
    C. Reasoning is the most important skill teaching.
    D. Reasoning is the most important skill taught.

22. A. You are not asking enough questions.
    B. You not asking enough questions.
    C. You are not to ask enough questions.
    D. You are not to asking enough questions.

23. A. She writing an essay.
    B. She is write an essay.
    C. She is writing an essay.
    D. She is to writing an essay.

24. A. He reading a book.
    B. He was reading a book.
    C. He was read a book.
    D. He to read a book.

25. A. We to read your book.
    B. We to reading your book.
    C. We want reading your book.
    D. We want to read your book.

Some verbs take infinitives as their objects and not gerunds. Others take gerunds as their objects and not infinitives.

✓ Verbs that Take Infinitives, and Not Gerunds, as Objects

agree	decide	seem
appear	hope	wish

- He *appeared to like* the cake.
- We *decided to talk* to the man.
- She *wished to eat* the raw fish.
- They *hope to go* to the show.

✓ Verbs that Take Gerunds, and Not Infinitives, as Objects

discuss	finish	mind
enjoy	keep	put off

- She *enjoys going* to the mall.
- He *put off speaking* to her.
- We *discussed reading* the story next week.
- I *finished telling* the story.

Exercise 12.2

Fill in. Fill in the blanks with the correct word form, gerund or infinitive, for the sentences.

1. She seems ____________ wearing red.
   (liking / to like)

2. We discussed ____________ to the lake last week.
   (going / to go)

3. She keeps ____________ the same airline to Chicago.
   (flying / to fly)

4. They finish ____________ by eight a.m..
   (eating / to eat)

5. John decided ____________ to the show with Henry.
   (going / to go)

6. Jill agreed ______________ about her favorite poem.
   (writing / to write)

7. Mike enjoyed ______________ with his friend.
(visiting / to visit)

8. Andrea wishes ___________ to Montana.
(going / to go)

9. The dog appears ___________ cared for.
(being / to be)

10. Sang-hee and Mike don't mind ________________ basic classes.
(teaching / to teach)

11. Henry didn't put off ______________ a song.
(writing / to write)

12. We were hoping _______________ the project this week.
(finishing / to finish)

13. I am deciding _____________ the test early.
(taking / to take)

14. The pants seem ____________ new.
(being / to be)

15. Children wish ______________ dessert.
(having / to have)

16. This class discussed ___________________ the test.
(putting off / to put off)

17. The children put off ___________ their homework.
(doing / to do)

18. The old men enjoy ______________ in the park.
(walking / to walk)

19. Did you agree ______________ for Sang-hee?
(waiting / to wait)

20. I decided ____________ with Sally.
(riding / to ride)

21. The cake finished _____________ in the oven.
(baking / to bake)

22. He kept ____________ in circles.
(going / to go)

23. The students hope _____________ an A on the test.
(getting / to get)

24. Susan appeared ____________ crying in class.
(being / to be)

25. I wish _________________ this exercise.
(finishing / to finish)

Practice saying the sentences.

Speaking Activity: In pairs, one partner ask the questions below. The other partner give answers using the same verbs and the correct choice of participles or gerunds. When you finish, switch roles.

1. When did you *decide* to major in your field?
2. Why did it *seem* to be a good major for you?
3. Did your parents *agree* to help you through college?
4. Did you ever *discuss* changing your major with your parents?
5. Have you *enjoyed* taking classes this semester?
6. Did you ever *put off* doing your homework?
7. Have you *finished* doing your homework this week?
8. Do your prospects *appear* to be good?
9. Do you *wish* to move to a big city when you graduate?
10. Where do you *hope* to work when you finish college?
11. Do you want to *keep* answering these questions?
12. Would you *mind* asking the questions now?

Reading. Below is an e-mail from a student informing a professor of an upcoming absence and requesting permission to write a paper on a specific topic.

Dear Dr. An:

My name is Jill Fitzpatrick, and I am a student in your 1:30 Tuesday-Thursday writing class. I am writing to tell you that I will not be going to class this Thursday. I am on the water polo team, and our coach is requiring our presence for an early practice that day.

So, I am following the instructions in your syllabus for absences. I understand that I cannot receive participation points for this absence. I am attaching the essay that is due on Thursday. In addition, I will be asking a friend to take notes for me for that day. Finally, once I have caught up with my friend, I intend to contact you with any follow-up questions I have.

I am also hoping to come and talk to you in your office next week about my research paper. Last week's class discussion about automation was interesting to me. We talked about how increasing automation frightened everyday working people who thought their jobs were going to be replaced by machines. However, the influence of industrialization on pop art in the 1960s is most interesting to me. I am an art history major, and I was hoping to be able to use what I've learned in my other classes as support for this research paper. I have written a paper on this before, last semester in Art History 125 with Dr. Bogosian. I was hoping to do further research, to update my findings, and to expand the paper to the necessary length for our class.

Thanks, and I will see you on Tuesday.

Yours sincerely,
Jill Fitzpatrick

Comprehension activity

1. What does Jill tell Dr. An about herself in the first sentence?
2. What excuse does Jill give for missing class?
3. What four things is Jill supposed to do when she misses class?
4. What was last week's class discussion about?
5. What topic is Jill interested in writing her research paper about?
6. What is Jill's college major?
7. What topic has Jill written a paper on for Dr. Bogosian?
8. Why does Jill want to do further research?
9. Which paper needed to be longer: the paper for Dr. Bogosian or the paper for Dr. An?

Writing Activity: Read the policy for absences on one of your course syllabi for this semester. Write an e-mail to that professor giving a reason for missing an upcoming class and explaining how you will accommodate the policy.